The Basics of Managing Finance in Educational Institutions

Sutapa Bose
Jayabrata Bose

ATLANTIC
PUBLISHERS & DISTRIBUTORS (P) LTD

Published by

ATLANTIC

PUBLISHERS & DISTRIBUTORS (P) LTD

7/22, Ansari Road, Darya Ganj,
New Delhi-110002
Phones : +91-11-40775252, 23273880, 23275880, 23280451
Fax : +91-11-23285873
Web : www.atlanticbooks.com
E-mail : orders@atlanticbooks.com

Branch Office
5, Nallathambi Street, Wallajah Road,
Chennai-600002
Phones : +91-44-64611085, 32413319
E-mail : chennai@atlanticbooks.com

Printed in India at Nice Printing Press, A-33/3A, Site-IV, Industrial Area, Sahibabad, Ghaziabad, U.P.

For Our Parents

Preface

Imparting education is the raison d'être of an educational institution, and effective management of the institution is the precondition for imparting education effectively. Management of educational institutions comprises management of various resources. Financial resource is crucial for running an organization. Hence, the ability to effectively manage an educational institution requires an understanding of the basics of managing finance.

Apart from the managers of educational institutions, the teachers also need to have a knowledge of the basics of accounting and financial management. This is primarily because of the emerging trend of 'shared governance' in educational institutions with teachers being an integral part of the governing body. Apart from carrying out academic responsibilities, teachers may also hold administrative positions in educational institutions. Those in schools may be head/principal, while those in institutions of higher education may occupy posts like chairperson, director, dean, registrar, vice chancellor and the like. Many would be the members of the finance committees and other decision-making bodies of their institutions. The knowledge of the basics of accounting and financial management may not be possessed by many teachers, academics and also educational administrators unless they have studied this discipline. Hence, for catering to the needs of educationists, academics and teachers of schools as well as of higher educational institutions, there is a pressing need for academic resource in this area.

There is no dearth of books on accounting, budgeting and other aspects of financial management but most of these books are meant for those from this discipline or aspiring to take up further studies in this area. Picking up such books, written for accountants and other finance professionals from the library and trying to understand the basics of financial management may be intimidating for teachers and educational managers from non-finance background. Thus, there is a need for a single source of information on all the aspects relevant for managing the financial resources. This book entitled *The Basics of Managing Finance in Educational Institutions* fills this gap. It does not try to convert teachers and educational managers into finance professionals but aims to introduce them to the pertinent aspects of this discipline. Moreover, it is well known that concepts, especially abstractions, are best learnt when they are contextualized. Keeping this in mind, unlike the books on financial management that are written in the context of the corporate world, this book is in the context of educational institutions. Another important feature of this book is that the principles of developing self learning material have been adhered to for designing and developing the content. There are ample scaffoldings, access devices, linkages within the content to facilitate navigation, objectives to keep learning focused and facilitate assessment, numerous examples to support explanations and suggested activities for gaining practical experience and stimulate reflection. It will prove useful to the teachers and administrators of schools, colleges and other educational institutions, particularly those who have to manage the financial aspects of such institutions.

Sutapa Bose
Jayabrata Bose

Contents

Sources of Funds and Resource Mobilization in Educational Institutions

1

1.1 Introduction

Financial resources are indispensable for operating an organisation and those providing education are no exceptions. The last few decades have witnessed a phenomenal growth in the number of educational institutions and consequently the rising demand for financial resources in the education sector. The number of universities has risen from just 28 in 1950-51 to over three hundred and fifty and the number of colleges grew from a mere 700 to over 15,000 in five decades of Independence. The student population has also exploded (Report of the Central Advisory Board of Education (CABE) Committee on Financing of Higher and Technical Education, 2005). By the end of the Tenth Plan in 2007, the Indian higher education system had grown into one of the largest in the world with 378 universities, 18064 colleges, faculty strength of 4.92 lakh, and an estimated enrolment of 140 lakh students (Eleventh Five Year Plan). As per the University Grants Commission there are in all 546 universities (including central, state, deemed and private universities) in India (http://www.ugc.ac.in/). As far as schools are concerned, 98% of India's rural population has access to primary schools within a kilometre of the habitation (Rath, 2008). Educational institutions are also finding it necessary to invest in aspects like an infrastructure that can support technology mediated functioning, modern laboratories, well stocked libraries, sports, auditorium and other facilities, and also, in qualified teachers and supporting staff, for providing quality education. No wonder, the expenditure on education has increased by several times during the last few decades.

Providing quality education to the masses requires adequate funds. Public investment has been the main source of funds for most of the educational institutions. In 1966, the Indian Education Commission, and thereafter in 1986, the National Policy on Education and the Programme of Action (1992) had recommended that the public expenditure on education should be 6% of GNP. Following the report of the Saikia Committee (1997) advocating free elementary education, in 1999, an expert group led by Tapas Majumdar, made estimates for additional fund requirements for universalizing elementary education. This committee analysed the financial implications of making elementary education a fundamental right and came to the conclusion that enhancing the investment to 6% of the GNP would be sufficient to provide adequate resources at all levels of the education system (Government of India, 1999 as cited in Geetha Rani, 2004). The National Common Minimum Programme of the United Progressive Alliance (UPA) government in 2004 and the Central Advisory Board of Education (CABE) committee in 2006 also made similar recommendations. However, actual expenditures in the education sector have never reached the targeted 6% of the GNP (De & Endow, 2008) but it has been all along considerably lower than this. The International Commission on Education for the 21st century (1996) said that as a rule of thumb in developing countries that have not yet achieved universalization of primary education, not less than 6% of the GDP should be devoted to education (Varghese, 2010). The government spending on education as percentage of GDP is just 4.1% in India, which is lower than even that made by countries like Kenya and Ethiopia (Ghosh, 2011). This naturally leads to the general perception on shortage of resources for education in India.

Owing to the inadequacy of public funds, coupled with growing financial needs, educational institutions are required to not only tap the sources of funds available but also mobilise resources. In this chapter, first the sources of funds available to educational institutions (schools and universities) have been described. Thereafter, the inadequacy of public funds and the ensuing need for mobilisation of resources in educational institutions have been presented. Following this the means for resource mobilisation have been elaborated. Towards the end the need for ethics in resource mobilisation has been highlighted.

1.2 Objectives

Following a study of this chapter, you are expected to:

- list the sources of funds generally available to educational institutions (schools and universities);
- describe the need for mobilising resources; and
- develop strategies for mobilising financial resources in educational institutions.

1.3 Sources of Funds

Education is indispensable for the development of a skilled workforce and thereby for human resource development. Hence, providing education is a responsibility of the government. The funds provided by the government, comprise the 'public funds'. India has a federal structure and education being a subject in the concurrent list of the Constitution, it is the responsibility of both the central as well as the state governments. Accordingly funds for education are provided by the central and the state governments, and also by the local bodies under the state government. For educational institutions, especially for those set up and or aided by the government, public funds, i.e. the funds provided by the government, are the main sources of funds. However, apart from public funds there are also private sources of funds, which may be tapped. The sources of funds for educational institutions—public as well as private have been discussed under two heads—sources of funds for schools and sources of funds for universities.

1.3.1 *Sources of funds for schools*

Elementary education since April 2010 is a fundamental right in India. Presently, India also aspires to universalise secondary education. To make these aspirations a reality and to provide quality education, the government has been the major provider of funds for school education. Funds may however, also be received from other sources in the form of endowments, land grants and the like. We shall first discuss the public funds.

1.3.1.1 *Public funds*

As mentioned earlier, funds received from the government comprise the public funds. The government runs/supports most of the schools in India. However there has also been growing participation of the private sector in the area of school education. Public funds are provided to not only government schools but also to the recognised aided private schools.

Funding by the central and state government

India has a federal structure and school education is funded to a great extent by the state government. Although both the centre and the states have a role in funding education in India but the states have the main responsibilities. The states provide grants to both public schools, i.e. schools run by the state government as well as to recognised aided private schools. Such grants may reach the schools directly or through local bodies. For aided private schools, land may be provided at subsidized rates by the local bodies. Government and government aided schools get grants from the Education Department of the state, while the state health department may provide service related to free health check up of students. The central government also provides grants for school education. Thus multiple authorities are involved in providing grants to schools. The fund from the central government is not received by the schools directly. It is usually routed through the state government. For schools systems like the Navodaya Vidyalayas, Kendriya Vidyalayas, Sainik Schools and the like, which are under the union government, funds are provided by the union government directly to the school systems.

The state government provides grants to the schools for different purposes like maintenance grants for the maintenance of the school plant, building grant for development and maintenance of the school building, equipment grants for the upgrading, maintenance and purchase of the equipments necessary for the school, salary grants for payment of salary to the school personnel, etc. Grants may also be provided to the schools so that they can meet their recurrent expenditure. Besides, there is also provision for providing special grants to selected schools in order to encourage them to perform activities for the welfare of the school/ society (Bhatnagar & Agrawal, 1997).

States fund education directly, the extent of which depends on their own revenues and priorities. States also receive central funds for education. The resource gap in the education funding of the state governments is partly met through transfers mandated by the Finance Commission from the central government to the states. This includes states' share in central taxes, non-plan grants and some conditional grants. The Planning Commission also provide the states with funds directly in the form of Central Assistance to States (used to support state plans) and indirectly through the Central Ministries in the form of Centrally Sponsored Schemes that flow to the district level (De & Endow, 2008). For instance, for the flagship educational programme, the Sarva Siksha Abhiyan (SSA) launched in 2000-2001, aiming to universalise elementary education in a mission mode, and prior to it, for educational programmes that were accorded high national priority like the Operation Black Board launched in 1987, the District Primary Education Programme initiated in 1994 and such other centrally sponsored schemes, funds from the central government are available. For implementing the fundamental right to education, the central government has proposed to share in a major way the financial burden to be incurred with the state governments. In spite of the moves towards decentralization of education, the share of centre in plan expenditure [plan expenditure is spent on productive asset creation through centrally sponsored programmes and the central government's flagship schemes like the SSA and non plan expenditure is such as that on maintenance of assets like the infrastructure (Singh & Mishra, 2010), payment of salary, etc.] in education has been increasing since the last three decades, and we may say that this trend has been significant after education was included in the concurrent list (De & Endow, 2008).

SSA provides various kinds of grants to schools with coverage up to the elementary level (grades 1st–8th). Three types of grants are mainly being provided: (i) Maintenance grant, for the upkeep of infrastructure; (ii) Development grant or School grant, meant for operation and administration; and (iii) Teaching Learning Material grant for instructional aids. The grants are provided with clear guidelines for expenditure. Grants may also be provided for expanding the school infrastructure by building additional classrooms.

Building grants provided for purchase and/construction of building for the school are subject to the approval of plan and estimates by the competent authorities. Maintenance grants are mainly for the maintenance of the school. For example, every year SSA provides maintenance grant for all government schools. The grants are usually meant for undertaking repairs needed in the school building. Schools with bigger infrastructure get more maintenance grants. Only through school management committees/Village Education Committees, maintenance and repair of school buildings may be carried out by schools.

Private educational institutions in India are of three main types: recognized and aided institutions, recognized but unaided or independent institutions, and unrecognized institutions. As mentioned by MHRD (1947-97), the recognized and aided institutions, in spite of being private institutions are treated as an integral part of the system of public education. Most of their expenditure comes from government grants and fees; and where fees have been abolished or are nominal the institutions depend almost exclusively on government funds. These institutions have a precarious financial position, partly because of the uncertainty of government grants and partly due to their own increasing incapacity to raise funds. Another problem is that the grant-in-aid rules being based on egalitarian principles, all private schools are treated alike for the purposes of financial assistance. This leads to limited funds for good schools while funds are wasted on non performing schools. Moreover, the grant-in-aid rules are generally complicated and difficult to administer and the amount of aid is inadequate. Consequently, most of these institutions have remained in a very unsatisfactory condition. Even now many private schools (aided ones) depend heavily on public funds.

Funding by local bodies

In USA financial support for public schools is provided at three major levels of government—federal, state and local governments (OrLosky, et al., 1984). In India also funds for education are provided at all these three levels. Local bodies like municipalities, corporations, and other bodies at the district and village levels provide funds to the schools out of the general body of funds available with them. Following two constitutional amendments (the 73rd and 74th Amendments), in 1993, more power has been given to rural and urban local bodies making them primarily responsible for education at the elementary level.

Funds from local bodies are usually referred to as local funds. The allocation of funds made by these local bodies is called local assignments, allotments or grants (Bhatnagar & Agrawal, 1997). Rural as well as urban local bodies are largely funded by the respective state governments. These local bodies may also spend resources that they may raise at their own level, from the local population on education. However, unlike the urban local bodies, in rural areas, own resources raised by the local bodies are a small proportion of their total revenue (De & Endow, 2008).

Types of grants

Grants to educational institutes especially schools are given on the basis of their approved expenditure which includes salaries paid to teaching and other staff, maintenance of buildings, rents, contingency expenditures, etc. Grants are usually consolidated amounts, which are determined on the basis of the requirements of the school concerned. Grants provided to schools are of mainly the following two types:

(A) Grants in Cash

(B) Grants in Kind

(A) Grants in Cash: Such grants are made in cash and some of the methods for calculating them, as given by Bhatnagar and Agrawal (1997) are:

- **Proportionate Grants:** Government gives a proportion, say one half or one third, of the approved expenditure of the school and the institution arranges the rest from different sources of income of the school. In case of one half of the approved expenditure being paid by the government, it is called "matching grants".
- **Gradation System:** This system of providing grants is based upon grading institutions in terms of their excellence. The institutions considered to be performing in a better manner are preferred in this system for giving grants.
- **Deficit Grant:** In this system grants are provided on the basis of the difference between the income and expenditure of the school. The grant intends to fill the gap between income and expenditure.
- **Multiple Systems:** Grants are provided on the basis of two or more of the above-mentioned systems say gradation system and deficit grant system taken together.
- **Capital Grants:** Such grants are given to meet the expenses that are to be incurred for a particular or specific purpose. It is not meant for general purposes. For example for building laboratories grants may be given to the schools.
- **Capitation Grants:** This is calculated on the basis of the number of students enrolled in the school. The schools with bigger student population receive more grants.
- **Fixed Grant System:** In this system the government provides a fixed amount to the schools and the rest of the expenses are met by the schools from their own resources.
- **Negotiable Ad-hoc Grant:** Such grants are given to tide over certain situations involving exigencies. For instance, due to a natural calamity if the school plant is destroyed,

the government may provide special grant to overcome the situation.

(B) Grants in Kind: These grants are in the form of material aids. For instance, technological gadgets like television, computers; laboratory equipments, books, meals for children, teaching aids, uniforms, bicycles for students, etc. that are provided by government/other agencies to schools are the examples of such grants.

A school has to be aware of its social obligations following the receipt of grants from public funds. This is true not only for the government schools but also for private schools receiving state aid. The private schools though are not under the direct administration of the government but condition for providing such schools with grants is that they fulfil the social obligations as well as maintain proper standards of education. For instance, following the implementation of the fundamental right to education in India, even private aided schools have been mandated to reserve a certain percentage of seats for the children from the financially weaker section and provide them with free and compulsory education till the elementary level.

1.3.1.2 *Private sources of funds*

Since fee, land grants, endowments and the like are obtained from sources other than the government, these funds are considered as private funds, which may be available to schools in the form of cash or kind. For example, for construction of school buildings, building materials may be donated by the community. Furniture, teaching aids, books for the library, computers and so on may be donated by various agencies. Unlike now, earlier, endowments and land grants, provided to educational institutions by the affluent people of the community were on a larger scale. Through such donations to schools, the donors sought the development of the schools and thereby of the community. Even now philanthropic organisations, trusts and individuals provide to schools financial help in the form of endowments and bequests, which could include financial aid, material aid and land grants. Many corporate houses including public sector organisations and even private organisations make such donations. Endowments benefit the schools by providing them with the means for growth, expansion and improvement. However, the stability of this source of funding is less than that of public funds. Moreover with the growing share of the government in funding education, this practice though continues but is no longer so prevalent (Bose, 2007).

Several states have invited private funds from individuals and the corporate sector. Rajasthan Government through its Rajasthan Education Initiative (REI) aims to engage global and local partners from the private sector, for multi-stakeholder partnerships to support quality education in the State. The REI has helped synergise the resources and opportunities in the government and the private sector to improve the access to quality education through ICT (Information and Communication Technology) and non ICT interventions (A Review of the Rajasthan Education Initiative (REI, 2009). Madhya Pradesh has also launched the scheme of "fund a school" that allows private funding of school.

Fees

Students of government schools and in some schools run by philanthropic bodies may pay nominal fees or even no fees. In some schools girls are exempted from paying tuition fees. Private schools usually charge higher fees than public schools. In private unaided schools, fees form the major source of funds. Tuition fees are collected either every month or after every three or four months. Not only the amount but also the type of fees charged varies with schools. Apart from tuition fee, building fees, library fees, laboratory fees, etc., which are the common types of fees, examination fees may also be collected before the term end examination, especially if it is conducted by a Board or University. Apart from fees, students may also have to make some monetary deposits that are refundable. For example, library deposits, caution money, etc. are refunded in case the student does not incur any liability towards the school by damaging or misplacing school property in the laboratory/library.

External Aids

External aid is also a source of funds in education. India's dependence on external aid, comprising loans and grants, has reduced with time. External assistance today plays more of a supportive role in financing major infrastructure projects, social sector projects (health and education) and in building up the institutional capacity (Government of India, 2008). Since the introduction of economic reforms in the 1990s, the nature and magnitude of funds from this source has changed considerably. International commitments to achieve education for all (EFA) in 1990s globally meant that India was an important case for donors. India was pressed to accept aid for primary education, and she agreed though with some reluctance. Thereafter for elementary education, from 7th Plan (1987-1992) when ₹ 81 million was the external aid utilized, it rapidly rose to ₹ 38,270 in the 10th plan (2002-2007) (Colclough & De, 2010).

In earlier years, education was financed mainly by domestic resources as aids focused on technical and vocational education. But external resources are now increasingly directed at elementary education. Following the "Education for All" conference in Jomtien in 1990, the international aid providers increased their aid commitments to primary education. There is also a significant portion of foreign aid both from foreign governments as well as from foreign private non-profit agencies (like Oxfam, Save the Children's Fund, etc), which does not flow through the government budgets. These agencies directly fund education in the Indian non-government organizations (Mehrotra et al., 2005 as cited in De & Endow, 2008).

Other miscellaneous sources of funds

Apart from public funds and endowments from private sources, there could be several other miscellaneous sources of funds like those listed below:

Fines: Fines are usually charged for late submission of fees and on disciplinary grounds.

Sale proceeds and rental: Schools may require students to purchase school uniforms, books, notebooks, stationeries and the like either from an outlet in the school's own premises or from those determined by the school. This is especially true for some private schools, which thereby get a share of the profit made by the agency concerned. School canteens run by the school itself or outsourced to an agency may also be a source of funds. Schools may earn funds by selling its products like those made by the science club like fire alarms, burglar alarms, ink, detergents, soaps, natural pesticides and fertilisers, products of art and craft classes, products of the horticulture cell, etc. Old newspapers and periodicals, furniture, sports items, laboratory items, and other materials no longer in use, may also be sold but as per the norms set by the management. Tickets sold during exhibitions, fairs, musical programmes, plays, sports and games organised by the school to parents and the community may also generate funds for the school.

Schools may allow the community to use its building and premises on holidays or after the working hours and charge money for it but in accordance with the norms developed by the management. For instance, examinations, halls may be let out.

Donations: While endowments may be provided voluntarily, schools may also seek donations from parents and the community. Donations may be sought in the form of cash or kind. This may be done for collecting funds for specific purposes like building an auditorium, developing sports facilities, organizing programmes like exhibitions, annual function, etc. In such cases the donors are convinced, either verbally during meetings or through a letter about the requirement, its exigency and the benefits that the students and the school would derive from it.

Interest from investment in financial institutions: The schools can invest the money it can spare in financial institutions for the growth of funds in case the financial rules of the institution permit such investment. However, the financial institution in which money is deposited needs to be chosen with care.

As indicated in Figure 1.1, there are several sources of funds and it is essential that funds provided by different agencies do not lie unused.

Future trends in funding

In India there has been a phenomenal increase in enrolment in private schools during the last few decades. There are studies indicating that many even among the poorer sections are preferring private schools for their children. This is mainly

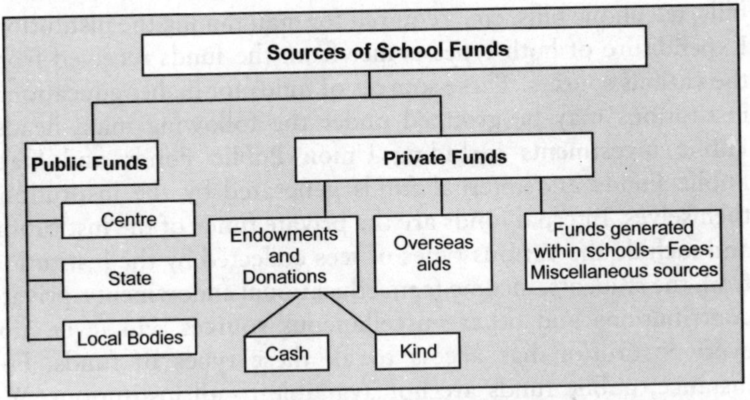

Figure 1.1: Sources of Funds for Schools

because of the failure of public schools to provide quality education, although providing quality education is one of the goals of the Governments' flagship programme, the SSA (Patnaik, 2006; "SSA fails to provide quality education", 2007; Aiyar, 2008). Hence, there are suggestions that instead of the present model of funds following schools, i.e. schools getting funds irrespective of their performance, funds need to follow students through educational vouchers provided to parents, who can then enrol children in schools of their choice. This is one of the ways to widen the range of schools from which parents may choose. This model adopted in countries like Sweden, Chile, Netherlands, Italy, etc. will make even the public schools competitive and there would be better utilisation of funds. Public private partnership is another model, which has been suggested to pool the resources of the government and the private sector for providing quality education. For instance, the infrastructure available with government schools and the quality of teaching and learning at private schools may be clubbed. In such a case the funding pattern may change.

1.3.2 *Sources of funds for universities*

Direct expenditure is a recurring expenditure unlike capital expenditure such as that made on infrastructure development. Direct expenditures of universities and colleges are mainly on recurring expenses incurred on salary, payment of electricity bills, telephone bills, etc., required for maintaining the institution. Expenditure of both types is met from the funds received from the various sources. These sources of funds for higher educational institutions may be grouped under the following main heads: Public investments including Union Public Funds and State Public Funds and internal funds generated by the institutions themselves. Internal funds are the private funds of the institution and include the various types of fees collected by the institution from the students, income from educational endowments, private contributions and other miscellaneous sources. However, not every institution has access to all these types of funds. For instance, publiç funds are not available to all institutions. We shall discuss it in the next subsection.

1.3.2.1 *Public funds*

The Universal declaration of human rights, (1948) says that everyone has the right to education .... and higher education shall be equally accessible to all on the basis of merit (Article 26). Higher education is of paramount importance for economic and social development (World Bank, 1994). It is indispensable for developing a skilled workforce. Students who attend institutions of higher education obtain a wide range of personal, financial, and other lifelong benefits. Apart from such personal gains, there are also social returns as the society as a whole derives a multitude of direct and indirect benefits when citizens have access to higher education (Baum & Payea, 2005). As per the Report of Justice Punnayya Committee (1993), higher education determines India's economic and technological progress. Hence, government funding must continue to be essential and mandatory requirement for supporting higher education and the government/state must continue to accept the major responsibility for funding it. In India while elementary education is Merit-1 good, post elementary education is Merit-2 good and hence, has to be financed considerable by the government/state [Report of the Central Advisory Board of Education (CABE) Committee on Financing of Higher and Technical Education, 2005].

As mentioned earlier, in India, education being in the concurrent list, it is the responsibility of both the centre as well as the states. Therefore, both the central as well as the state government are involved in financing higher education. Funding for higher education (universities) is done mainly through the grants-in-aid system. The University Grants Commission (UGC) is the main agency that provides grants. Also, the specialised agencies of the government such as the Council of Scientific and Industrial Research (CSIR), Indian Council of Social Science Research (ICSSR), etc. may provide funds for activities like research.

The central government is responsible for formulating and implementing the major policies relating to higher education. It provides grants to the UGC and establishes central universities. It is responsible for declaration of Educational Institutions as 'Deemed to be University' on the recommendation of the UGC. The central government plays its part through the Ministry of Human Resource Development (MHRD), which has the Department of Higher Education. One of the objectives of MHRD is 'planned development' of university and higher education and of technical education in the country (http://www.education.nic.in/uhe/uhe.asp). State governments are responsible for the establishment of state universities and colleges, and provide plan grants for their development and non-plan grants for their maintenance. The share of the state public funds provided by the state government is much more than that of the central government in higher education.

In the field of higher education as in school education, among all the sources of income, public fund is the main source of income. But in private institutions, income from fees is much more than that of state run institutions. However, the income from endowment has been coming down over the years. Therefore, it is rightly said that massive public investments and reducing private investments characterise funding in higher education in India.

Role of the University Grants Commission (UGC) in funding

The UGC is mainly responsible for allocating and disbursing funds provided to it by the Central Government to universities and college level institutions. UGC provides grants-in-aid to bridge the difference between income and expenditure of universities. It provides Development (Plan Grants) as well as Maintenance (Non-Plan Grants). It may inquire into the financial needs of universities for allocating and disbursing grants from its fund. UGC provides grants to universities established or incorporated by or under a Central Act for the maintenance and development of such universities or for any other general and specified purposes. It also allocates and disburses grants from its fund to other universities as it may deem necessary or appropriate for their development or maintenance or both, for any specified activities of such universities or for any other general and specified purposes. However, for releasing any grant to such universities, UGC gives due consideration to the development of the university concerned, its financial needs, the standard attained by it and the national purposes that it may serve. It also allocates and disburses from its funds grants to institutions that are deemed to be universities, as it may deem necessary for maintenance and in special cases, for development and for any other general and specified purposes. However, no grant shall be given by the central government, the UGC or any other organisation receiving funds from the central government to any university that has been established after the UGC (Amendment) Act, 1972, unless UGC is satisfied and declares that the university is fit for receiving grants.

UGC financially assists those eligible colleges, which are included under Section 2(f)

> The UGC had notified Regulations for recognition of colleges under Section 2(f) of the UGC Act, 1956. The colleges are brought under the purview of UGC as per the provisions contained in these Regulations as and when proposals are received from the colleges for inclusion under Section 2(f) and subsequent to their being found fit for inclusion as per the Regulations and thereafter declared fit to receive central assistance (UGC grant) under Section 12 (B) of UGC Act, 1956 as per approved pattern of assistance under various schemes.

Although, among the colleges included under Section 2(f)/12(B) of UGC Act 1956, many have been declared eligible to receive central assistance, including UGC grants under Section 12(B) of UGC Act 1956 but the remaining colleges though are recognized under Section 2(1) of UGC Act 1956, are not declared as fit for receiving central assistance as these institutions do not fulfil the conditions laid down for attaining such a status (http://www.ugc.ac.in/inside/ugc_recog_college.html).

The UGC receives funds from the Ministry of Human Resource Development (MHRD). It releases funds under different heads/schemes. The grants provided are mainly of the following two types:

- Development (Plan) Grants
- Maintenance (Non-Plan) Grants

Plan grants are generally for growth, diversification and innovation to be carried out by an institution and non-plan grants are meant for the maintenance of the institution. All activities that are of recurrent nature, taken up during a five year plan period, following the plan are classified as non-plan or maintenance activities. Non-Plan assistance is provided to universities to meet the recurring expenditure on salaries and for maintenance of infrastructure and for other expenses like telephone bills, electricity bills, etc. Central universities and colleges affiliated to them and institutions deemed to be university by the UGC receive both the plan and non-plan grants. However, the state universities and their affiliated colleges receive only plan grants for improving the infrastructure and basic facilities, attaining excellence in teaching, research, etc.

Development (Plan) grants is provided basically to improve the infrastructure and basic facilities so as to achieve at least the threshold level and to develop excellence in those universities which have already made good progress. Development assistance is provided for teaching as well as for technical staff, equipments like laboratory equipments, modern technological equipments for educational purposes, furniture, books and journals, construction as well as repair of building, development of campus, health centres, amenities for students such as canteens, recreational facilities, counselling, etc.

Funding Central Universities: Central universities are established by the MHRD, usually by an Act of Parliament. Maintenance grant provided to an institution is determined on "covering of deficit" basis, i.e., the internal receipt of the institution is deducted from the actual expenditure incurred in any financial year and usually out of this amount a reserve cannot be built up. This amount varies from institution to institution and usually an incremental increase is made every year. Development grants are sanctioned for activities such as expansion and for developing new programmes by the institution.

Funding State Universities: A state level university is set up by an act of State Legislature. As stated earlier Section 12(B) of the UGC Act, says that State Universities established after 17th June, 1972 shall not be eligible to receive any grant from the Central Government, UGC or any other Organisation receiving funds from the Government of India, unless UGC satisfies itself, as per the prescribed norms and procedures, that such a university is fit to receive grants. Although development of state universities is primarily the concern of state governments, development grants, including grants under special schemes, are provided to all eligible state universities by the UGC. Such grants facilitate the creation, augmentation and upgradation of infrastructural facilities that are not normally available from the State government or other sources of funds. Apart from these development grants, state universities are also provided with additional grants under different schemes like, jubilee grants, special one time grant for upgrading existing laboratories and libraries, etc.

Grants for higher education are of different types. Plan funding may be as Infrastructure Grant based on campus size, programs offered, number of departments/faculties, expansion plan for increasing student numbers and program diversification, etc. Performance Grant is given on the basis of research and consultancy, continuing education, support to technical education system at large and industry, etc. Special grant may be based on factors like age of the institutions, campus size, etc.

The UGC has a scheme that will be in operation during the current XI Plan (2007-2012). Under this scheme it will provide General Plan Development Grants to individual universities (Central, State and Deemed) on the basis of outlays determined and communicated to the universities. The grants are aimed at the consolidation of infrastructure and modernising teaching, research and administration and for activities meant for responding to the changing needs. It has listed certain aspects like increasing access, ensuring equity, imparting relevant education, improving quality and excellence, enhancing facilities for students, augmenting research, etc. under the development scheme. For meeting these objectives, financial assistance would be provided to universities under heads such as infrastructure: buildings, campus development, staff, central library, innovative research activities, ICT requirements, health care, student amenities, jubilee grants (for having completed 25, 50, 60, 75 and 100 years), etc. (http://www.ugc.ac.in/financialsupport/xiplan/guideline.html#univ).

There are still many institutions that do not receive any grants or get only meagre amounts. The expenditure on higher education in India as percentage of GDP remained stagnant over the last few years as 0.37%, while in countries like USA, UK and China it is about 1.41%, 1.07% and .50% respectively. Majority of funds go to only 130 out of 1,80,000 institutions. The rest either do not receive funds or are allocated only small amounts ("Higher education spend stagnates", 2007). Thus public investment in higher education is much lesser than that required. The government is unable to finance higher education to the desired extent because of the growing numbers of colleges and universities and universalization of elementary and now secondary education requiring huge amounts of resources. The eleventh plan envisages UGC grants for over 8000 degree colleges and over 170 Universities, which are not receiving UGC grant at present and 50% sharing basis—to be strengthened to get eligibility for 12B recognition under UGC Act (Implementation of major initiatives in Higher Education in the XI Plan, MHRD).

Professional councils also play an important role in higher education. They are responsible for recognition of courses, promotion of professional institutions and providing grants to undergraduate programmes and various awards (http://www.ugc.ac.in/inside/pcouncil.html).

In India as in many other countries there is negotiated funding. This is done on the basis of the funds received in the previous year and making some increase to it. This is an incremental approach. The actual funds provided however, depends on factors like availability of funds, extent of requirements, negotiating skills of the institution, etc. This approach gives the funding body some degree of control over the recipients. The problem arises when there is a scarcity of resources, which makes allocation uncertain. Also, within this method of covering the deficit, those performing better are treated at par with non performers.

In 1992, the UGC had set up a committee under the chairmanship of Justice Dr. K. Punnayya to examine the financial situation of central universities, deemed universities, colleges affiliated to Delhi University and Banaras Hindu University, and the technical institutions funded by the Government of India. The committee was also asked to make necessary recommendations and suggest methods to determine their financial needs and to suggest changes, if any, which could be introduced in the system of grants provided to these bodies in future. The recommendations of the Committee on funding include the following:

Input funding: Funding is related to inputs and establishes a relationship with cost and efficiency. Cost parameters consider student-teacher ratio, staff-student ratio, space allocation, etc. and develop a set of cost inputs adopting weighting system relating to funding, depending upon the requirements of funding authorities. This approach promotes cost consciousness and accountability.

Output funding: Institutions are paid for their output, in terms of graduates and post graduates. This covers both costing and partly, efficiency factors.

Student funding: Institutions are more or less free to fix the fees and the state would fund the students, to meet their tuition and living costs. Funding of students may be based on merit. It could be combined with the requirement of social justice. Funding for tuition fees and living costs could be separated and living costs linked to economic criteria. Student-based funding may ensure cost effectiveness and quality. But it could lead to development of different levels of institutions based on quality and cost factors.

1.3.2.2 *Private sources of funds*

In the previous section we have discussed public funds for universities, and the funding agencies. In this section, we shall discuss the private funds for universities. Some sources of funds lie within higher educational institutions such as fees, endowments, etc. These are the private or internal sources of funds. Due to inadequacy of public funds, the government of India has been urging institutes of higher education for generating private funds. The government constituted committees to examine the issue of mobilisation of resources for central universities.

A committee was set up under the chairmanship of Justice K. Punnayya (UGC, 1993) and thereafter for technical education, under the chairmanship of Dr D. Swaminadhan, Swaminadhan Committee (AICTE, 1994) was set up. Committees were again formed by the UGC to specifically, look into the recommendations of the Punnayya Committee on unit cost of higher education, under the chairmanship of Dr. M.V. Pylee (UGC, 1997); to review the norms of maintenance grants for Delhi Colleges under the chairmanship of Dr. Anandakrishnan (UGC, 1999) and to formulate the revision of fee structure under the chairmanship of Dr. Mohammad-ur-Ruhman (UGC 2000). These committees urged higher education institutions to generate private funds. It was suggested that universities need to tap internal sources of funds and generate internal resources which should be sizeable in course of time (Geetha Rani, 2004).

Although these committees recommended fee hike, there are still restrictions regarding the fee to be charged for institutions receiving public funds, especially in government run institutions.

Endowments are receding. Hence the internal source of income for government educational institutions is often quite low. Nevertheless they are important. The major sources of internal funds are the following:

Fees

The fees collected are one of the sources of income of institutions offering higher education. Unlike in government institutions, in private ones, the fee happens to be a major source of income. Capitation fee charged by some private institutions though has been banned by the Supreme Court in 1992, but fee charged by self financing institutions is still higher than government institutions. Different types of fees are charged by institutions offering higher education. Apart from tuition fees, there could be special Non Resident Indian/foreign student fees, fee for merit and payment seats, admission/registration fee, examination fee, laboratory fee, library fee, hostel fee, fee for special services like change of address, early declaration of results, re-evaluation of answer scripts, etc. Fee has to be paid either on a one time basis or periodically. Apart from fees, students may also be required to make certain types of monetary deposits that are refundable. For instance, caution money for laboratory, library deposits, etc. is refunded following the completion of the course, provided the student does not incur any liability towards the institution.

Over the years income from fee had been coming down. The committees set up for resource mobilisation, which we have just mentioned were in agreement on the need to hike fee as it constituted an important source of internal funds and also because it was felt that there had not been upward revision of fee since a long time. It was felt that since, the continuation of the present level of subsidy benefits even those who can afford non subsidized education, hence, increasing fees to mobilise resources has been recommended by these Committees. Hence, an urgent need for substantial upward revision of fees by universities and colleges was recommended. Swaminadhan Committee (1994), set up for technical institutions recommended resource mobilisation in technical education, essentially through cost recovery from students. One of its recommendations was enhancing fees to recover at least

20 per cent of the recurring expenditure. Mahmud-ur-Rahman Committee Report (2000) set up specifically to formulate the revision of fee structure said that the Universities are expected to generate at least 15 per cent of their recurring expenditure at the end of every five years and 25 per cent at the end of every 10 years. This committee proposed upward revision of various types of fees, not just tuition fees, but also of examination fees. It recommended that the fees be in two broad categories—tuition fees that would cover the actual cost of imparting education and developmental fees. It was also suggested that tuition fee may be revised upwards with immediate effect and it may be periodically adjusted keeping in view the inflation and rise in costs of higher education. The revision of fees must be related in a meaningful manner to the recurring cost of the course of study and employment opportunities offered by the particular course. Thus courses leading to greater job opportunities should have higher fees. A differential fee structure was thus suggested (UGC, 1993).

With regard to fees for admission and examination, the committees recommended the recovery of the recurring cost of operations. For facilities like library, laboratory, sports and the like, it was suggested that these fees must be revised to recover a significant part of the recurring cost (UGC, 1993). It was also recommended that the development fee be revised to meet the actual recurring cost on no-loss-no-profit basis (UGC, 1999; 2000 as cited in Geetha Rani, 2004). For hostel and mess fees, it was recommended that these fees should meet the actual recurring cost and cover part of the capital cost over time (UGC, 1993; 1999; 2000 as cited in Geetha Rani, 2004). The general perception is that fees are extremely low and they have not been revised for decades, but this is actually not so. The reality is that most universities have not revised fee like tuition fees, but welfare services meant for students like hostel, water, electricity, food charges and the development fees have been revised to a substantial extent (Geetha Rani, 2004). Still the total fee charged in government institutions is much less than that charged by private institutions.

Fee hike may be uniform across educational programmes or different programmes may be priced differently and professional programmes may be priced higher. However, this system does not discriminate among different paying capacities. Therefore, discriminatory pricing of higher educational services has been vouched by many. This implies that instead of subsidising higher education for every one, those capable of paying should be charged higher fees. The rationale behind it is that higher education is availed mostly by those who are economically better off and hence subsidising their higher education is not required. Hence, students incapable of paying higher fees may be exempted. This has been put into practice in some institutions through fee concessions offered to certain categories of students.

Endowments

As mentioned, earlier, endowments are the financial assets given by the community to the educational institutions. They are usually aids in the form of cash or kind. Besides helping the individual students, endowments benefit the organisations by providing them with the means for growth, expansion and improvement. Corporate houses, philanthropic organisations, alumni, trusts set up for funding institutions of excellence and even individual donors may contribute funds to educational institutions. These funds are often used for new projects, research, upgrading technological facilities, developing infrastructure, scholarships to students, etc. With increasing government funding of education, there has been a decrease in the funds received as endowments and bequests.

Endowments help in enhancing financial autonomy, but stability in this source of funding is less than in public funds. During phases of economic slowdown, even première educational institutions may face fall in endowments from the corporate sector and philanthropists. In the USA, Moody's, a credit rating agency had predicted that although higher education has been more insulated from economic impact in prior recessions but 2009 will be a rough year as donations, financial aid, and other grants would fall as state governments and philanthropists reel from the economic downturn (Clark, 2009).

Other miscellaneous sources of funds

Funds may be available from miscellaneous sources like sale of assets, interest from corpus funds, donations, funds accruing from renting of infrastructural facilities for examination, conferences, etc., consultancy fee, sale of journals, sale of in-house publications like courseware, subscription received for journals published by the institution, etc. The Indian government's stand on external aid as stated earlier has been of reluctance in receiving aids for education. Still, external aids provided by governments and international organisations like the United Nations (UNDP, UNICEF, UNESCO), Common Wealth of Learning, World Bank are also available for funding certain projects or activities undertaken by universities.

The trends in the financing of higher education in India show that while the share of the government in total educational expenditure has increased substantially over the years; but the share of higher education in the total public education expenditure has declined, both in plan allocation and in recurring expenditure. There has also been a decline in student fees and endowments (Varghese, 2000). Unlike in technical education where the union and state governments have almost equal financial responsibilities, in case of higher education, the union government shares only 30% of the total government expenditure. In the 10th Five Year Plan it was expressed that the part of the problem facing universities is the inadequate funds from the government. Public investment in higher education is only 0.4% of the GNP while many developed nations spend about 1.0-2.5% of their respective GNP. Due to inadequacy of funds, escalating costs and increasing needs of the system, higher education in India is in a deep financial crisis. As a result several universities and institutions of higher education face severe financial constraints (Report of the CABE Committee on Financing of Higher and Technical Education, 2005). This can take a serious toll on the quality of education provided. The 11th Five Year Plan, hailed as India's education plan, has proposed 19.8% of its outlay for education with an outlay of ₹ 84,743 crores for higher education, which is much more than that earmarked in the tenth plan. Consistency in this approach in the subsequent plans is required.

1.4 Mobilisation of Resources

The word 'mobilisation' means setting into motion or movement, bringing into circulation, and the like and mobilisation of resources, for this chapter, implies generating financial resources by educational institutions. Financial resources are indispensable for providing quality education. We have mentioned earlier about the inadequacy of government funds, which happens to be the main source of finances for educational institutions owned by the government. The government's education expenditure as a percentage of GDP has never ever risen above 3-4% of GDP in India, while in countries like Cuba it is a double digit figure. Although long back the Kothari Commission (1964-66) and much later the XI plan (2006-2010) proposed almost double the amount, i.e. 6% of the GDP and during this plan there has been some increase in the provision. Still the provision made for education is grossly inadequate and more so in comparison to the developed industrial nations average annual expenditure of 5-6% of their GDP for education (Thakore, 2010).

We have mentioned in the previous section that off late because of shortage of public funds higher education institutions have been urged for self sufficiency and this is apparent from the recommendations of the various committees set up by the government. Even schools are advised to mobilise resources (Commonwealth Secretariat, 1993). The scope of this chapter restricts a debate on the advisability of this issue. But now that a stand has been taken that educational institutions, especially those offering higher education need to generate revenue, educational institutions need to be 'edupreneurs' (a term coined by combining education and entrepreneurs). In this section, we shall discuss the strategies that may be adopted by educational institutions for resource mobilisation.

First we shall focus on resource mobilisation in schools and thereafter in institutions of higher education.

1.4.1 *Mobilisation of resources in schools*

Schools have needs beyond that for basic infrastructure and human resources. There is need for communication technologies that assist educational activities, library, laboratories, playground, equipments for sports, art, craft and music, facilities for medical examinations, guidance and counselling services, etc. Hence, besides utilizing the grants in a judicious manner, there is also the need for creativity, dynamism and entrepreneurship on the part of the school principal, teachers and students for generating funds in addition to the grants received. Although funds may not be generated in substantial amounts and the school will still remain dependent on the inflow of other sources of funds, nevertheless any amount generated can take care of some needs.

A school head today cannot afford to sit back and wait for more financial grants. S/he is the team leader and the representative of the school. S/he is the person who has the authority and power to organize fund raising activities. Moreover, being the team leader s/he can inspire the staff and the students and impress upon the community the need for funds for providing better education. S/he has to lead his/her team in exploring and tapping the different sources of funds that could be made available for the school (Bose, 2007).

Strategies for resource mobilisation

The Eleventh Five Year Plan says that even in public schools, there is a need to encourage levy of some fees for students for enabling school management to raise resources for quality improvement but this should be accompanied by a generous provision of scholarships to those who cannot afford such fees, particularly girl students who are at the risk. However, with the attempts to universalize elementary education and now with education, becoming a fundamental right, levying fee or fee hike may hardly be the solution for resource mobilisation. Therefore, there is a need to explore other means of mobilising resources at the school level.

As suggested by Singh (2008, as cited in Burt, 2010), schools while providing education at economic rates can generate their own resources, and improve the relevance of education they provide rather than relying on external financing or user fees. But how can one mobilise resources? A school does not function in isolation but has a symbiotic relationship with the community. Hence, it is the community in which lies the sources of funds and the key to the mobilisation of resources is to involve the community. Generating funds through sale proceeds, investments and donations are dependent on the community. In India, the Janshala model (the globally acclaimed programme, wherein five UN agencies UNICEF, UNDP, UNESCO, ILO and UNFPA joined together with the governments to improve the quality of education by involving the community), which adopted an open and community based approach for achieving universal elementary education aimed to mobilise the resources within the community.

The resources generated may not only be in cash but also in kind like land, materials for construction and the like. It is difficult to provide an exhaustive list of the techniques through which schools may generate funds. This is because fund generating actives are to be carried out in the context of the school and the community. Situations in rural schools are different from those of an urban school. Again, factors like the competencies available in the school and the resources of the community are important for planning resource mobilisation activities. However some activities that have been suggested in the Section 1.3.1.2 like generating funds through sale proceeds and rentals, appealing for donations, getting interest on investments made, may be initiated.

A school provides education and thus ushers in socioeconomic growth of the society. Therefore, the school head should not shy away from appealing for donation and endowments for the school. Advertisements about the achievements and activities undertaken and those to be undertaken by the school may be placed in the local dailies along with an appeal for financial help. Old newspapers and magazines from the library, equipments and furniture no longer in use and other such materials may be sold off as per norms set by the management of the school, at regular intervals to generate funds instead of wasting space in storing them.

There is need for planning in advance and preparing a schedule of resource mobilisation activities to be held during a calendar year and responsibilities may be delegated to the team of teachers and students formed for this purpose. In the absence of well thought out activities, investments may go waste. For example, investment in horticultural inputs may be futile if climatic and soil conditions are overlooked. The involvement of the community in planning activities, providing expertise and also as end users could be helpful.

Schools engaging in activities for mobilisation of resources will have the following benefits:

1. There will be planned production and sale of goods and services in accordance with the in-house capabilities of the school and the need of the community.
2. An indirect benefit of resource mobilisation would be training in entrepreneurship for students.

> The Fundación Paraguaya—a Latin American NGO committed to poverty elimination through entrepreneurship set up an upper secondary school, the San Francisco Agricultural School, at Paraguay (South America) for youths aged 15-19, with a focus on agriculture. The Fundacion Paraguaya aimed to generate its own funds and become financially self-sustaining, instead of awaiting funds from external sources like the government, donors or even by charging high fee from students. Besides maintaining self-sufficiency, the school has two other laudable missions. One is to equip students with agricultural skills, and thus enable them to be successful agricultural extension agents, who are empowered by the education they receive to start their own food enterprises, or they can disseminate knowledge of beneficial agricultural methods to the members of their own communities. Another mission is to promote and replicate the model of a self-sufficient agricultural school elsewhere.

The school thus sets a new model of providing high-quality technical/vocational education at a low cost to students who are mainly from the economically disadvantaged section. This type of Self-Sufficient Schools approach is an innovative methodology that integrates technical-vocational education with entrepreneurship developed through small-scale, on-campus rural enterprises. The school-based entrepreneurship imparts skills not just in the subject concerned but also in marketing strategies. This approach connects classroom practices to real world needs and thus enhances the relevance of education. It is thus a model which offers a rich training ground for students in the subject as well as in entrepreneurship. This model was recently selected by UNESCO as a "best practice in youth policies and programs." Many institutions in Latin America and Africa are adopting this model.

Sources: Burt (2010); Community Food Enterprise: Local Success in a Global Marketplace (2009); BBC World Challenge 2008-Agricultural School of Paraguay (http://www.youtube.com/watch?v= pIQJLRlQEL0&feature=youtube_gdata)

In schools activities related to horticultural, farming, art, craft, like clay work, embroidery, cultural programmes and sports are common. Proficiency in these activities coupled with marketing skills develops in students the ability for self-employment and entrepreneurship. Teachers may guide students in selecting activities that are relevant in the context of the school and the community and thereafter in planning and carrying out such activities as small scale enterprises (Commonwealth Secretariat, 1993).

1.4.2 *Mobilisation of resources in institutions of higher education*

There has been a phenomenal growth and expansion of higher education since independence. There has also been a growing involvement of the public sector in higher education, while the share of endowments, i.e. in financing institutions of higher education has been coming down. Hence, the state has been the main funding agency for education. Elementary education naturally gets priority over other levels of education. Elementary education receives about half of the total budgetary expenditure. Following the allocation of a relatively lesser but still substantial amount for secondary education, higher education including technical and other professional education is therefore not left with much. Hence, most states have encouraged private investment in technical and other professional sectors since the past several years.

Empowerment of higher education requires funding, which has been far from satisfactory (Report of the CABE Committee on Financing of Higher and Technical Education, 2005). Declining share of higher education in the total public education expenditure both in plan allocation and in recurring expenditure indicates the reduced public priority and resource commitment towards higher education, especially in the late 1980s. You have read earlier that in the 1990s, the Government of India set up Committees to come out with solutions for the problem of funding higher education and the suggestion of these committees to mobilize resources from non-governmental sources to sustain the system of higher education. We have already discussed this aspect in the section 1.3.2.2.

The recommendations of the Punnayya Committee (1993) include: (i) maintenance grants, dearness allowance to be provided by the government; (ii) subsidies on many of the other items of maintenance grant to be reduced and maintenance grants to be stabilised at a certain acceptable level; (iii) maintenance grant to be based on unit costs; (iv) universities to mobilise funds—at least 15% of the total recurring expenditure at the end of the first five years and 25% at the end of 10 years; (v) creation of corpus funds to meet infrastructure development; (vi) increase in student fees keeping in view the rate of inflation; (vii) scholarships to at least 20% of students; and (viii) soft loan scholarships from nationalised banks (Varghese, 2000). You have already read that similar recommendations for financial self sufficiency had been made by the other committees appointed during this period. The reform measures suggested by the World Bank (1994, as cited in Varghese, 2000) for developing countries also include similar recommendations, which are: (i) encouraging greater differentiation of institutions of higher education, including development of private institutions; (ii) cost-recovery mechanisms including cost-sharing with students; (iii) redefining the role of the government by evolving a policy framework to make the sector more market friendly and public institutions more autonomous; and (iv) prioritising investments towards quality improvement.

Punnayya Committee (1992-1993) had linked cost consciousness, efficiency and accountability to funding. Later Swaminadhan Committee had similarly urged the need for improving efficiency in the functioning of institutions of higher education by reducing wastage and saving resources. Thus the need for mobilizing resources by institutions from private sources was suggested by several committees set up during the nineties, the World Bank and later even by the National Knowledge Commission (NKC) (2006). As per the (NKC) (2006) the expansion of our system of higher education is not possible without enhanced levels of financing. While public financing should rise to 1.5%, the rising expenses must necessarily be met by both public and private sources. Besides, other possibilities that can complement the public expenditure need to be explored. It suggested that first of all the government needs to adopt steps that would make education cost effective. Although it may be an unpopular step but the subsidy enjoyed by students may be lessened. The beneficiaries of higher education, the students themselves and the future employers could shoulder the responsibility of funding. Apart from rationalization of fee as has been often recommended, ensuring a return from those graduating in the form of tax or cess imposed on them could plough back funds into the public funding system. Another option could be loans from the other beneficiaries of higher education, the employers. Prospective employers may provide loans to learners. A similar view point is also reflected in the approach paper to the Tenth Five-year Plan and the Tenth plan document. These documents say that as budget resources are limited, and resources available, need to be allocated to expanding primary education, it is important to recognise that the universities must make greater efforts to supplement resources from the government (Government of India, 2001, 2002-2007, as cited in Geetha Rani, 2004). Hence, it is clear that the factor of cost-effectiveness and returns are, extremely relevant to the present-day concept of higher education as an investment.

The idea of reducing public investment in education, though still being debated and is not welcome by many, is not new. Long back, the noted economist, Alfred Marshall (1890, as cited in Stokes & Wright, 2008) in Principles of Economics had said that if the investment in higher education system could produce one more Newton or Darwin, Shakespeare or Beethoven, the public spending would have been justified. Hence, the responsibility of financing education should not be borne solely by the government, but also by the individuals/parents and the employers in the proportion of the benefits reaped by them.

There is a need to take the recommendations for fund mobilisation by institutions offering higher education seriously because decreasing per student real expenditure on higher education by the government affects the quality of education. Cost cutting measures like hiring part time teachers, having faculty smaller than that required, compromising on infrastructure and enhancing enrolment without proportionately increasing faculty and infrastructure and the like take a heavy toll on the quality of education provided. Due to inability to pay lucrative salary, best teachers are not attracted. As stated by the NKC (2006) many colleges have crumbling buildings, decrepit laboratories and hardly any amenities for students. There is a serious resource crunch in universities which leaves them with little financial flexibility. About 75 per cent of maintenance expenditure is on salaries and pensions. Of the remaining 25 per cent, at least 15 per cent is spent on pre-emptive claims such as rents, electricity, telephones and examinations. The rest, which is less than 10 per cent, is not even enough for maintenance let alone development. Laboratories, libraries, and buildings are in poor state. Moreover, in most universities, plan (investment) expenditure is less than 5 per cent of non-plan (maintenance) expenditure. It is therefore felt that the society has to bear the cost of higher education as it used to do earlier, if not entirely, at least substantially. Hence, the institutions themselves will have to involve the community and offer such services that will generate resources. Therefore, institutions providing higher education need to have entrepreneurship skills. In the past, activities undertaken for generating funds was considered to be leading to commercialisation of institutions and hence looked down upon by institutions of higher education. Today the outlook is changing and building a healthy partnership with the society and pursuing activities that mobilise resources from the community is no longer considered sacrilegious.

Means for mobilisation of resources

NKC (2006) said that the government financing will remain the cornerstone of any strategy to improve the system of higher education but State financing, however, would not suffice for the massive expansion in higher education that is an imperative. Therefore, it is essential to explore a wide range of possibilities. Some means for resource mobilisation as suggested by the NKC (2006) have been elaborated.

Better asset management: NKC (2006) urged universities to have an innovative asset management plan, in consonance with their objectives. Untapped assets of universities like surplus and unused land could be put to good use. Using surplus land for agricultural/horticultural purposes or selling or leasing out unused land can bring revenue to the institution.

Rationalisation of fee: Punnayya Committee and Swaminadhan Committee had also recommended cost recovery by higher education institutions. This implies lessening subsidies on higher education, and shifting the incidence of the financial obligations of the government to the beneficiaries, i.e. the students and also the future employers. Graduate tax to be paid by employers of manpower that has been educated by the state and enhancing fees are some of the mechanisms to implement it.

To support students to pay higher fee, there could be student loans. But insistence of loan providers for collaterals may debar poor students of this facility. But collateral is necessary after a certain limit. This is because as with other loans, if the credit giving agencies are allowed to take collateral, the fear of non payment by students after graduating will not withhold lending.

As per the data compiled by the Indian Banks Association, the number of students applying for educational loans has doubled across the country during the last five years. This indicates not just the increase in the number of aspirants for higher education but also the relaxation of educational loan norms. While educational loans were earlier mainly available to the meritorious, now even those with average performance can avail loans. There is also no collateral required for loans up to a considerable amount. Loans are mainly applied for professional programmes like engineering, management and now even for teacher training programmes ("No. of edu loans doubles in 5 yrs", 2011).

Although various committees recommended upward revision of fees, but as far as capitation fee is concerned, the Supreme Court in 1992 had practically banned capitation fee charged by private educational institutions, saying that charging capitation fee was unreasonable, unfair and unjust. In 1993 in the UnniKrishnan vs. State of Andhra Pradesh case the Supreme Court had although said that education is a fundamental right and cannot be used for profit making, but it introduced differential fee system in private institutions, with free seats for the meritorious and payment seats for others (Michael & Kretovics, 2005). In October 2002 in the TMA Pai Foundation vs. the State of Karnataka case, the Supreme Court advised that the revenue surplus which may be generated by the educational institution should be invested for the purpose of development of education and expansion of the institution. It was also said that the fees to be charged by unaided institutions cannot be regulated but no institution should charge capitation fee.

The NKC (2006) said that on an average, fees constitute less than 10 per cent of total expenditure in our universities. And, in most universities, fees have remained unchanged for decades. Universities refrain from rationalizing fee mainly because of concerns regarding access and also to some extent because it would not be welcomed by the students and the people in general. But low fee often benefits the unintended beneficiaries, the students from well to do families. Universities should do a rethink and go for rationalization of fees. Universities may decide the level of fees but, as a norm, fees should meet at least 20 per cent of the total expenditure in universities. Fees also need to be adjusted every two years through price indexation. Such small, continuous, adjustments would be absorbed and accepted far more easily than abruptly introduced large, discrete changes after longer periods of time. You will find that these recommendations are in line with those made by the committees set up in the nineties by the Government of India, we have mentioned earlier. Rationalisation of fees as per NKC however, should be subject to two conditions: first, students from economically weaker sections should be provided with a fee waiver plus scholarships to meet their costs; second, universities should not be penalized by the UGC for the resources raised from higher fees through matching deductions from their grants-in-aid.

Fee hike though recommended for mobilising resources, if unregulated, it may make education a business rather than a service to the nation and may deepen inequalities as those who cannot afford high fees will be deprived of higher education.

International Students: In ancient times educational institutions of India like Nalanda drew students from abroad. Now a huge number of Indian students go abroad for higher education every year. Universities of certain developed countries are pumping in billions of dollars into their economies through fees paid by foreign students. Such outflow expands access to higher education but also results in outflow of funds. If students from abroad can be drawn into our system, funds would flow in. Just as Indian medical services are considered to be economic but efficient and people even from many developed nations come for medical tourism, seeking medical care, similarly institutions offering higher education could try to attract foreign students. As suggested by the NKC (2006) India is not an attractive destination for international students, not even as much as it used to be 30 years ago. It is required to make a conscious attempt to attract foreign students to India for higher education. This would enrich our academic milieu, enhance quality and would be a significant source of finance.

An Indian case–Indira Gandhi National Open University (IGNOU)

IGNOU provides educational services in 40 countries. An International Division has been established in IGNOU to put into operation the international role of IGNOU. IGNOU is now offering programmes in various disciplines like Social Sciences, Education, Management, Computer Sciences and Information Technology, Commerce, Library and Information Sciences, Tourism Studies, Nursing, etc, IGNOU first made its international presence felt abroad in 1994 by making available its Post Graduate Diploma and Master's Degree programmes in Distance Education to the students in 19 Commonwealth countries across Asian, African, Pacific and Caribbean countries under the COL-Rajiv Gandhi Fellowship scheme.

In 1996 the International Cell (International Division of IGNOU was established on 16th October as a Cell and was upgraded to a Division in 2002) was assigned the task of promoting the delivery of the academic programmes of IGNOU by establishing bilateral and multi-lateral co-operation and exchanges at the international level. The university subsequently opened centres in 40 countries. Currently IGNOU's academic programmes are on offer in Abu Dhabi, Dubai, Sharjah, Doha, Kuwait and Sultanate of Oman among the Gulf countries; Maldives, Mauritius and Seychelles among the Indian Ocean Island nations; Ethiopia and Liberia in Africa in collaboration with International Institute in Capacity Building in Africa (an UNESCO organization); Vietnam in collaboration with Hanoi Open University, in Myanmar in collaboration with University of Distance Education, Myanmar and in Singapore and a few other countries. This is a testimony to the demand in foreign countries for higher education offered by an Indian university (*Source*: www.ignou.ac.in).

Many universities, including private ones like Sikkim Manipal University, are also drawing foreign students. Just as many developed countries aggressively advertise and participate in educational fairs to canvass their educational services, the same could be done by Indian institutions. In view of globalisation and rising interest in India due to her steady economic growth and political stability, studies on Indian culture and languages could draw students from other countries. Also, the curriculum may be developed with a global perspective to draw international students.

Philanthropic contributions: This has come down over the years and philanthropic funding is getting scarce. Earlier it was not so. Calcutta University, Annamalai, Madras University and many others were the recipients of generous philanthropy from industrialists and also communities. Genuine philanthropic commitment can transform India's higher education and research space (Mehta, 2010). In fact, the proportion of such contributions in total expenditure on higher education has declined from more than 12 per cent in the 1950s to less than 3 per cent in the 1990s. It should be possible to nurture this tradition of philanthropy through changes in incentives for universities and for donors (NKC, 2006).

Donations should be encouraged by educational institutions and the government has to see that it does not affect the grants received, rather award them with matching grant in aid. It was also felt that other related regulations that deter endowments should also be removed. In this regard, the Punnayya Committee had recommended that there should be 100% income tax concession on all endowments and contributions made to universities and additional concessions to donors sponsoring research projects in universities. The government has accordingly implemented this and now there is 100% exemption to donors and another 25% for funding approved research projects (Ghosh, 1997).

> In keeping with the recommendations of the Punnayya Committee (1992-1993), the UGC has evolved a scheme entitled "Incentives for Resource Mobilization". This scheme basically intends to develop a healthy partnership between the university and the society so that they participate and contribute to the growth of each other. It urges universities to mobilise resource from the society. It also urges universities to provide consultancy on payment basis to industries, the government and other bodies on vital issues. The scheme also includes provisions for incentives by making a contribution against the financial contributions received in the preceding financial year by the universities which succeed in their efforts at such external resource mobilisation

Encouraging investment by the private sector: Educational institutions may make efforts to encourage private investment in lieu of professional services provided by the learners during their internship or after passing out. The private sector may also be allowed to have chairs in universities for funding activities related to it. It is essential to stimulate private investment in higher education as a means of extending educational opportunities. This is because government financing cannot be enough to support the massive expansion in opportunities for higher education on a scale that is now essential (NKC, 2006).

Public-Private Partnerships: Robust public-private partnership can not only bring in funds but also improve the quality of higher education. Partnership of public funded institutions with private agencies like industries, education providers and the like willing to make (not-for-profit) private investment can lead to mutual benefits. Institutions like, Tata Institute of Social Sciences, Tata Institute of Fundamental Research, Indian Institute of Science are centres of excellence involving such partnerships. It might be possible to leverage public funding, especially in the form of land grants, to attract more (not-for-profit) private investment. As suggested by NKC (2006), in principle, it should be possible to set up new institutions in higher education, as public-private partnerships where the government provides the land and the private sector provides the finances. Such public private partnerships which promote university-industry interface would also strengthen teaching and research. However, there has also been criticism for public-private participation approach. The Planning Commission's Approach Paper towards education sector in the 12th Five Year Plan calls for developing the education sector on the basis of public-private partnership (PPP). This approach has been criticized as the private sector may be interested in making profits, while educational institutions should not be run for profit ("12th Five Year Plan approach to education draws flak", 2011).

Obviously, universities must not be driven by commercial considerations. But it would be prudent to tap other sources such as alumni contributions, licensing fees, or user charges (for facilities in universities used by people from outside) (NKC, 2006). The Punnayya Committee (1992) had also recommended that for generating income the universities should let out their infrastructural facilities like playgrounds, auditoria, etc. and also organize short term courses for which there is demand. They should also solicit endowments, contributions and actively participate in consultancy without affecting the academic activity of the institutions. The other ways are to undertake continuing education programmes by the various departments to generate income for the university, form alumni associations and get donations from them and the like. A university-industry interface also helps as the industry benefits by the consultancy and research carried out by the institutions and the latter gets funds. It is also to be remembered that money saved is money generated. Hence, economy in running the institutions is required. Long term and short term investments of surplus funds also bring money in the form of interest (Ghosh, 1997).

Institutions may have in their governing board participation from the corporate world. There may also be financial incentives for joint industry-university research, corporate-sponsored internships for students, and of professionals from the industrial sector. This kind of nexus between academic institutions and industry not only makes the curriculum relevant but may also assure students with placement following the completion of the course.

Offering courses with demand in market: Courses that have demand in the market are being offered by private institutions, especially in the field of professional education. Courses on technical and management education and also on teacher education are offered by many private institutions. Multi-disciplinary and inter-disciplinary short term courses that are tailor made to serve market demands are offered by many private institutions and even government ones like IGNOU. Unlike the conventional university courses, these courses are more in demand.

Off late not only self financing institutions but many public funded institutions are also offering self financing courses. Consultancy services may also be provided to industries, agricultural and animal husbandry firms, etc. Courseware can also be marketed. For example, IGNOU markets its courseware in print medium as well as that in audio and video media. Providing online education to a global target has generated huge amount of funds for many universities and this can be done by Indian universities too. Interest earned on financial investments, is also a means for generating funds.

Today fund seekers are numerous. Several NGOs, various kinds of institutions, individuals in various capacities are actively seeking funds. Universities and institutions of higher education therefore need to adopt well thought out and sound strategies that convince the donor. Resource mobilisation requires special talent and it is true that there is an acute shortage of professionally skilled manpower for resource mobilisation in universities and other educational institutions. As discussed for schools, a committee headed by the leader of the institution may be formed for this to plan and develop strategies necessary for resource mobilisation.

1.4.3 *Ethics in resource mobilisation*

Ideally education is to be provided with the sole motive of providing social service but growing needs coupled with shortage of funds in educational institutions are becoming the compelling reasons for resource mobilisation. Still it is difficult to strike a balance between the idea of education as a social service and that of fee hike. There is perhaps also a thin line between commercialisation of education and fee rationalisation for resource mobilisation by the institution, leading to steep fee hike. Even while adopting other means for resource mobilisation, howsoever acute the need may be it has to be kept in mind that funds should not be generated in an unethical manner and never with profiteering motives. Nor should education be a financial burden on students, especially for those disadvantaged.

Mobilising funds through exorbitant fees or repeated requests for donation, forcing purchase of uniforms, books, etc. from shops that charge much more than others would not retain the *not for profit* nature of a school. Educational institutions need to see that the fees charged and the contributions sought do not pose a burden on the student/parents. Some private institutions, especially schools raise funds by the sale of items like stationeries, books, uniforms, etc. through designated outlets and by organizing services for children like school bus services, providing training in music and sports after the school hours, etc. However, if high profit margin is maintained or poor quality services are offered, there would be exploitation of the recipients of the service/goods. During fairs, festivals, cultural programmes organized by educational institutions with paid entry for the community, the institution has to be careful that activities/ events do not cease to be aesthetic and are suitable for educational institutions. If premises are rented out, it should be seen that those who are hiring it do so for socially acceptable purposes. Finally, funds may be generated not just for the sake of increasing the capital but also for utilising them judiciously for the development of the institution and mainly for the welfare of the students (Bose, 2007). The bottom line is that fund generation has to be the means of development and never an end in itself.

Fund raising need to be based on certain principles such as the following:

- All resource mobilisations should be within the legal frame work. No illegal activities can be undertaken.
- Funds cannot be raised from illegitimate sources.
- Financial exploitation of students and parents has to be avoided.

- Funds raising activities and the utilisation of the funds raised should have accountability and transparency in the entire process.

1.5 Summary

Sources of funds for educational institutions are of two major types—public and private. The former is provided by the government, while the latter is generated internally by the institutions. For schools, public funds are provided as grants by the central and the state government and at times even by local bodies to educational institutions. Although both the centre and the states have a role in funding school education in India but states have the main responsibilities and provide grants to both public schools as well as to recognised aided private schools. States fund education directly, the extent of which depends on their own revenues and priorities. States also receive central funds for the centrally sponsored educational schemes like the SSA. Funding for universities is mainly through the grants-in-aid system. Both the central as well as the state government are involved in financing higher education but the share of the public funds from the state government is much more. The UGC plays an important role in providing grant-in-aid to all universities established by a Central Act and also to some of those established by the states and to the institutions deemed by it as universities to bridge the difference between income and expenditure of universities. It provides Development (Plan Grants) as well as Maintenance (Non-Plan Grants). It may inquire into the financial needs of universities for allocating and disbursing grants from its fund. However, not all institutions are eligible for such government grants.

Among the private sources of funds for schools and higher education institutions, off late, endowments have been receding. Although private education institutions, especially those offering higher education have been disallowed from charging capitation fees, still in private institutions, fee brings in a substantial amount of funds, unlike in the public institutions. External aid is also a source of funds in education though India's dependence on external aid has reduced with time. Educational institutions may also tap funds from miscellaneous sources like sale proceeds from goods produced/services rendered to the community, by letting out premises, interest on money deposited in financial institutions and the like.

Phenomenal expansion in the field of education coupled with rising expenses required for providing quality education have led to a steep increase in the demand for financial resource for providing quality education. But public investment, which has been the main source of funds for most of the educational institutions falls far short of the amount recommended. Due to the huge gap between desired level of funds and that actually available, there is a need for tapping not only the potent sources of income, but also undertake resource mobilization.

In view of the resource crunch and rising expenses in education, several committees set up by the government in the nineties, as well as the NKC (2006) urged institutions offering higher education to mobilize resources. It was also decided that UGC would not provide lesser grants but rather offer incentive for resources mobilized.

Schools are also being urged to mobilize resources. In schools horticulture, farming, art, craft, cultural programmes and sports may be used for resource mobilisation. Essentially the means of mobilizing resources are similar in schools and in institutions offering higher education. However, fee hike for mobilizing funds in schools, is not recommended. For higher education institutions, the NKC (2006) suggested some means for resource mobilization viz. better asset management for putting into effective use untapped resources of the institution, fee rationalization but with consideration for students from the weaker sections, drawing in international students, encouraging endowments and investment by the private sector and public-private partnerships. Besides these, marketing educational services and courseware, offering self financing courses, etc. are some of the measures that can be adopted.

Educational leaders and teachers have to be creative and innovative in mobilising resources for the institution. Well planned strategies with proper implementation are needed and to encourage and monitor such activities, the authorities may themselves take lead. However educational institutions should not become commercial organizations while mobilising funds and should never resort to unethical means. Mobilizing resources should therefore remain only as the 'means' for the development of the educational institution and not be an end in itself because in such a case it would amount to profiteering, which is not the aim of education providers.

1.6 Self Assessment

1.6.1 *Questions*

(i) Explain the role of the government in funding schools.

(ii) Critically examine the role of the government in funding universities.

(iii) Differentiate between plan and non plan grants.

(iv) Do you think educational institutions need to devote time and efforts in mobilising resources? Justify your answer.

(v) Describe some of the ways to mobilise resources in schools.

(vi) Describe some of the ways to mobilise resources in higher education institutions.

1.6.2 *Clues*

(i) Public funds are provided to not only government schools but also to the recognised aided private schools. In India states have the main responsibilities regarding funding schools. It provides grants to the schools for different purposes like maintenance grants, building grants, equipment grants, etc. (for details see Section 1.3.1.1).

(ii) Both the central as well as the state government are involved in financing higher education but the state has the main responsibility. Funding for higher education (universities) is done mainly through the grants-in-aid system. The University Grants Commission (UGC) is the main agency that provides grants. It allocates and disburses funds to universities and college level institutions. However, the public funds are far from being sufficient (for details see Section 1.3.2.1 and 1.4.2).

(iii) Plan grants are generally for growth, diversification and innovation to be carried out by an institution and non plan grants are meant for the maintenance of the institution (see Section 1.3.2.1).

(iv) Decreasing public investment, growing needs that are to be fulfilled for quality education (for details see Section 1.4).

(v) Selling goods produced in schools through horticulture, art, craft, letting out premises, investments, etc. (for details see Section 1.4.1).

(vi) Fee rationalization but with consideration for students from the weaker sections, drawing in international students, encouraging endowments and investment by the private sector and public-private partnerships (for details see Section 1.4.2).

1.7 Activities

You may carry out these activities for gaining a better understanding of this chapter.

1. Visit a few schools as well as institutions of higher education that receive government grants. Discuss with teachers and the institution head to find out about the types of grants received and their adequacy for the institution concerned.
2. Discuss with teachers of schools and colleges to find out their views on the need for resource mobilisation in their institution and whether activities for resource mobilisation are carried out. If yes, find out the means adopted.
3. Draw a sample of students studying in private schools. Interview their parents to ascertain their views on the efforts made by the school for mobilisation of funds from parents.
4. Draw a sample of students studying in private colleges. Interview them to ascertain their views on the fee charged by the institution. Find out whether they are satisfied with the educational services provided.

References

A Review of the Rajasthan Education Initiative (REI) (September, 2009). By the Global e-schools and communities initiative (GeSCI). World Economic Forum. Retrieved on 22.8.11 from http://www.gesci.org/assets/files/REI%20Report.pdf

AICTE (1994). *Report of the High Power Committee for Mobilisation of Additional Resources for Technical Education* (Dr. Swaminadhan Committee Report), All India Council for Technical Education (AICTE), New Delhi.

Aiyar, Y. (2008, January 23). A report card for India. *The Indian Express*. Retrieved on 12.5.08 from http://www.indianexpress.com/printerFriendly/264472.html

Baum, S. & Payea, K. (2005). The benefits of higher education for individuals and society. Education pays 2004. *Trends in higher education series, Collegeboard*. Retrieved on 7.9.11 from http://www.collegeboard.com/prod_downloads/press/cost04/EducationPays2004.pdf

BBC World Challenge (2008). Agricultural School of Paraguay. *Youtube*. Retrieved on 7.9.11 from http://www.youtube.com/watch?v=pIQJLRlQEL0&feature=youtube_gdata

Bhatnagar, R.P. & Agrawal, V. (1997). *Educational Administration, Supervision, Planning and Finance*. Surya Publications: Meerut..

Bose, S.(2007). Source of School Funds. *School governance and financial management*. PG Diploma in School Leadership and Management. New Delhi: IGNOU.

Burt, M. (2010). *Self-Sufficient Schools: Fostering Entrepreneurship to Finance Sustainable Education*. Paper presented at the First International Development Conference of Syria, organised by the Syria Trust for Development, Damascus 23-24 January 2010. Retrieved on 24.9.11 from http://syriadevconf.org/sites/default/files/1-1%20martin%20burt_0.pdf

Clark, K.(2009, January27). The Recession Hits College Campuses: It could be a "turning point" in how much it costs to attend college. *US News Education*. Retrieved on 27.9.11 from http://www.usnews.com/education/articles/2009/01/27/the-recession-hits-college-campuses

Colclough, C. & De, A. (2010). The Impact of Aid on Education Policy in India *Research Consortium on Educational Outcomes and Poverty* (RECOUP) Working Paper No. 27. Retrieved on 25.8.11 from http://recoup.educ.cam.ac.uk/publications/WP27-CC_ADfinal.pdf

Commonwealth Secretariat (1993). *Better Schools, Resource Materials for School Heads in Africa*. Module 5—Financial Management. Commonwealth Secretariat, UNESCO: London.

Community Food Enterprise: Local Success in a Global Marketplace (2009). *A Project of the Wallace Center at Winrock International and the Business Alliance for Local Living Economies*. USA: Wallace Center at Winrock International.

De, A. & Endow, T. (2008). Public Expenditure on Education in India: Recent Trends and Outcomes *Research Consortium on Educational Outcomes and Poverty (RECOUP) Working Paper* No.18. Retrieved on 19.8.11 from http://recoup.educ.cam.ac.uk/publications/WP18-ADfin.pdf

Eleventh Five Year Plan, Social Sector, Volume II. Planning Commission, Government of India. New Delhi: Oxford University Press. Retrieved on 25.8.11 from http://education.nic.in/plan/XIPlandocument.pdf

Eleventh Five Year Plan Document on Education, MHRD. Retrieved on 25.8.11 from http://planningcommission.nic.in/plans/planrel/fiveyr/11th/11_v2/11th_vol2.pdf

Geetha Rani, P. (2004). Economic Reforms and Financing Higher Education in India. *Indian Journal of Economics and Business* 3(1), pp 79-102. Retrieved on 12.9.11 from http://ijeb.com/Issues/data/June04_6_erafheii.pdf

Ghosh, D.K. (1997). *Financing education resource generation in education.* India: Cosmo Publications.

Ghosh. J. (2011, July2-15). *Frontline*. Retrieved on 22.8.11from http://mrzine.monthlyreview.org/2011/ghosh290611.html

Government of India (1997). *Compilation on 50 years of Indian Education: 1947-1997*. Ministry of Human Resource Development, Department of Education with National Informatics Centre. Retrieved on 11.10.07 from http://education.nic.in/cd50years/r/2S/99/2S990701.htm

Government of India (1999). *The report of the expert group on financial requirements for making elementary education a fundamental right* (Chairman, Prof. Tapas Majumdar). New Delhi: Ministry of Human Resources Development.

Government of India (2001). *Approach Paper to the Tenth Five-Year Plan*: 2002-2007. Planning Commission, New Delhi.

Government of India (2002-2007). *Tenth Five-year Plan: 2002-2007*. Planning Commission, New Delhi.

Government of India (2008). *Position paper on external assistance received by India*. Ministry of Finance, Department of Economic Affairs, Project Monitoring Unit. Retrieved on 25.8.11 from http://finmin.nic.in/the_ministry/dept_eco_affairs/pmu/PositionPaper_ExtAssist.pdf

Government of India (2007-2012). *Eleventh Five-year Plan: 2002-2007*. Vol.2. Planning Commission, New Delhi.

Higher education spend stagnates. (2007, January 6). *The Economic Times*. Retrieved on 12.9.11 from http://economictimes.indiatimes.com/higher-education-spend-stagnates/articleshow/1068280.cms

Increased literacy is good but improve education quality too: Experts. (2011, April10). *The Economic Times* Retrieved on 20.9.11 from http://articles.economictimes.indiatimes.com/2011-04-10/news/29403327_1_literacy-rate-growth-rate-quality-of-school-education

Marshall, A. (Ed). (1890, 1920). *Principles of Economics*. Macmillan and Co, London.

Mehrotra, S., Panchamukhi, P.R., Srivastava, R & Srivastava, R. (Eds.). (2005). *Universalizing elementary education in India: uncaging the tiger economy*. New Delhi: Oxford University

Mehta, P.B. (2010, October 19). Charity at home? *The Indian Express*, New Delhi.

Michael, S.O. & Kretovics, M. (Eds.). (2005). *Financing higher education in a global market*. New York: Algora Publications

National Knowledge Commission, Government of India (2006-2009). *Report to the Nation.*

National Knowledge Commission (2006). *Note on higher education*. Retrieved on 26.9.11 from http://knowledgecommission.gov.in/downloads/recommendations/HigherEducationNote.pdf

No. of edu loans doubles in 5 yrs (2011, September12). *The Times of India*, New Delhi.

OrLosky, D.E., McCleary.L.E., Shapiro, A. & Webb D.L. (1984). *Educational Administration Today*. New York : Mcmillan Publishing Co.

Patnaik, I. (2006, May16). What Arjun should focus on? We need qualitative improvement in government schools not more quotas. *The Indian Express*. Retrieved on 15.9.07 from http://openlib.org/home/ila/MEDIA/2006/ssa.html

Rath, A.K. (2008). Girls' education in India: achievements since independence. Press Release, 23.1.2008. Ministry of Human Resource Development. Retrieved on 20.2.08 from http://pib.nic.in/release/release.asp?relid=34844&kwd=

Report of the CABE Committee on Financing of Higher and Technical Education (2005), NIEPA Retrieved on 24.8.11 from http://www.education.nic.in/cabe/Report%20CABE%20Committee%20on%20Financing%20Higher%20and%20Technical%20EducationL.pdf

Saikia Committee (1997). *Report of the Committee of State Education Ministers on Implications of the Proposal to Make Elementary Education a Fundamental Right*. New Delhi: Ministry of Human Resource Development, Department of Education (Chairman: MuhiRam Saikia).

Singh M., (2008). *School Enterprises Revisited: Combining Vocational Learning with Production in Work. Learning and Sustainable Development.* Netherlands: Springer.

Singh, S. & Mishra, A.R. (2010, October18). Distinction between non-plan, plan expenditure may end soon. Economy and Politics. Livemint.com & *The Wall Street Journal*. Retrieved on 14.9.11 from http://www.livemint.com/2010/10/18232805/Distinction-between-nonPlan.html

Sulochana, M. (1991). *Financial management of higher education in India*. Allahabad: Chugh Publications.

Stokes, A. & Wright, S. (2008). Measuring the social rate of return in public sector labor markets. *Journal of Business & Economics Research*, 6 (5). Retrieved on 27.9.11 from http://journals.cluteonline.com/index.php/JBER/article/view/2413

SSA fails to provide quality education (2007, September16). *The Economic Times*. Retrieved on 4.10.10 from http://economictimes.indiatimes.com/News/News_By_Industry/Services/Education/SSA_fails_to_provide_quality_education/articleshow/2373522.cms

Thakore, D. (2010). Sixty-third disappointment for Indian education. *Education World The human Development Magazine*. Retrieved on 4.10.10 from http://www.educationworldonline.net/index.php/page-article-choice-more-id-2195

12th Year Plan approach to education draws flak (2011, September 30). *Indian Education Review*. Retrieved on 4.10.11 from http://www.indiaeducationreview.com/news/12th-year-plan-approach-education-draws-flak

UGC (1993). UGC Funding of Institutions of Higher Education, *Report of Justice Dr. K. Punnayya Committee, 1992-93*, University Grants Commission, New Delhi.

UGC (1997). *Report of the Pylee Committee on the Recommendations of the Punnayya Committee Relating to Unit Cost of Higher Education and Other Issues*, University Grants Commission, New Delhi.

UGC (1999). *Report of Dr. M. Anandakrishnan, Expert Committee appointed by the University Grants Commission to review the Maintenance Grants Norms for Delhi Colleges*, University Grants Commission, New Delhi.

UGC (2000), *Report of the Committee Constituted by UGC for Formulation of Revised Fee Structure in the Central and Deemed Universities in India*, University Grants Commission, New Delhi (Dr. Mohammad-ur-Ruhman Committee).

Varghese, N.V. (2000). Reforming education financing. Seminar, Vol. #494, Unviable Universities, October, 2000. Retrieved on 15.9.11 from http://www.eledu.net/rrcusrn_data/Reforming%20education%20financing.pdf

Varghese, N.V. (2010). Strategies for financing education: Public funding and changing aid modalities *Journal of Educational Planning and Administration*. XXIV (3). Retrieved on 13.10.11 from http://www.nuepa.org/Download/Publications/JEPA%20July%202010%20(Sample%20issue).pdf

World Bank (1994). Higher Education: The Lessons of Experience, Washington D.C. Retrieved on 26.9.11 from http://siteresources.worldbank.org/EDUCATION/Resources/278200-1099079877269/547664-1099079956815/HigherEd_lessons_En.pdf

Websites

http://www.education.nic.in/uhe/uhe.asp Retrieved on 28.9.11

http://www.ugc.ac.in/inside/ugc_recog_college.html Retrieved on 28.9.11

http://www.ugc.ac.in/financialsupport/xiplan/guideline.html#univ Retrieved on 28.9.11

http://www.ugc.ac.in/inside/pcouncil.html Retrieved on 28.9.11

www.ignou.ac.in/ Retrieved on 28.9.11

http://www.ugc.ac.in/ Retrieved on 28.9.11

Accounting

2

2.1 Introduction

In the previous chapter you have studied the sources of funds and about the need and means for resource mobilization in educational institutions. How can we keep track of fund inflow tapped from various sources and how to keep track of their outflow? This chapter introduces you to yet another important aspect of financial management—accounting. Maintaining accounts as you may already know is essential in all profit making organizations. But what about those that do not function with the motive of making profits but nevertheless have an inflow and outflow of funds? Even such organizations, that are also called not for profit or non-trading organizations, require maintenance of accounts for sound economic decision making and financial management. Educational institutions are supposed to be not for profit organizations. As managers of an institution offering education, you are neither expected to maintain accounts yourself nor become an expert in accounting. Nevertheless a basic idea about accounting will help you in carrying out your managerial functions, especially if you are not from this field. Therefore, in this chapter you will be introduced to the basics of maintenance of accounts. This will empower you in your efforts towards supervision of not only accounting in your institution but also enable you to carry out the other functions related to financial management such as budgeting, internal and external auditing (to be discussed in the next chapter) and thus in better financial decision making and overall financial management. As you read this chapter you will realize that 'accounting', though may sound difficult to many who have not studied it, is after all not so difficult. In this chapter, we have presented the basic concepts associated with accounting in a stepwise manner. We have discussed first the need for accounting, thereafter the major concepts and conventions of accounting and then the processes involved.

2.2 Objectives

Following a study of this chapter, you are expected to:

- explain the concept of accounting;
- explain the concepts and conventions in accounting; and
- describe the steps of accounting process.

2.3 What is Accounting?

Irrespective of the nature of an organization i.e. whether it is a business organization or a non-trading concern like an educational institution, recording the day-to-day financial transactions is essential. This is mainly because such a practice helps to track the inflow and outflow of funds on a daily basis and helps in ascertaining the financial position of the institution on a particular date. However, recording the financial transactions has to be a systematic process and follow the generally accepted principles and guidelines for accounting. Before you proceed, it is necessary for you to have an idea of two concepts namely book keeping and accounting. The main objective of these two processes in an educational institution is to keep track of inflow and outflow of funds.

Bookkeeping: In order to run an educational institution it will be necessary to carry out a large number of financial transactions depending upon the size of the institution. It is humanly not possible to remember all the transactions. This necessitates recording these transactions. Bookkeeping is the process of recording the financial transactions in the books of accounts. This activity is however of mechanical nature and does not involve any analysis of the impact of the financial transactions. As mentioned by Shukla (2004) bookkeeping involves regularly recording in financial terms, all financial transactions like purchase, payments, receipts, sales and the like carried out by an organization according to certain rules and with certain objectives. It is a simpler process in comparison to accounting and provides records of day to day financial transactions for accounting.

Accounting: You are surely familiar with this term but what does it actually mean? The sphere of accounting starts where the bookkeeping ends. Accounting involves the preparation of reports and the interpretation of reports. The scope of accounting is wider than book-keeping, because besides recording, it also involves summarizing (preparation of financial statements), interpreting financial transactions and communicating operating results to the various stakeholders. Accounting is based on a combination of principles, rules, postulates of accounting and also personal judgments. It involves specialized knowledge of rules on the basis of which, records of daily business transactions are kept in a systematic manner (Gupta, 2004). You may read yet another definition of accounting, according to which accounting has been aptly referred to as the 'Language of the Business' as it is used to communicate the financial performance of the organization to various stakeholders. It is basically concerned with the collection, recording, classification and presentation of financial data to serve the purposes of the management and other stakeholders and even the government (ICWAI, 2003). You will understand the concept of accounting better when you read in the subsequent sections how accounting is done.

Need for accounting

Why undertake accounting at all? Educational managers as well as other stakeholders would need to maintain accounts with the basic objective to have a clear and comprehensive picture of the financial situation of the organization. This is essential because of the following reasons:

- To record all financial transactions of the organization in a permanent manner.
- To have financial records that are essential for analysis of the financial information, which helps in planning and decision making for the ongoing and future activities of the organisation.

- For ascertaining the financial position in terms of income and expenditure of the organization in general and also for specific activities.
- The investors (government/private bodies), management, donors, suppliers, lenders, government agencies like taxation authorities, employees, agencies involved in planning, and policy making are able to acquire the necessary financial information about the educational institution concerned.
- To assess the financial performance during a given period.
- To know the financial position in terms of assets and liabilities on a particular date.
- For controlling expenditure and planning for augmenting the sources of income through exercises pertaining to resource mobilization.
- To facilitate financial reporting.
- To facilitate filing of tax returns—payroll tax return, i.e. return in respect of deposit of tax deducted at source, which may be important for an educational institution.

There could be other reasons too which you may determine and add to this list.

In an institution, including one for imparting education, you will find that accounting of financial transactions is done usually with two basic objectives: Primary and secondary objectives that have been summed up through the following diagram (Figure 2.1).

2.4 The Accounting Equation

An account helps in maintaining and tracking financial transactions, i.e. amounts an individual(s)/organisation owns/owes/spends/receives. For instance we have savings accounts in banks, which indicate the money the bank owes us; for the loan you take from an organisation, there will be accounts that indicate the money you owe to it. A financial transaction indicates the flow of money from one account to another account. This may happen when an individual/organisation spends or receives funds with ensuing transfer of money between accounts. Accounting centers

OBJECTIVES

PRIMARY OBJECTIVES

- To record all financial transactions on permanent basis
- To prepare final accounts i.e. Income & expenditure Account and Balance Sheet at the end of an accounting period
- To ascertain operational results i.e. excess of income over expenditure & vice versa and financial position at the end of an accounting period.

SECONDARY OBJECTIVES

- To facilitate budgetary estimates
- To maintain records with a view to prevent and detect fraud, errors and wastage
- Providing information to management and other stakeholders

Figure 2.1

Source: Bose & Agarwal (2007)

around five basic aspects of an institution (Figure 2.2) namely Assets (the economic resources which the institution owns as for instance, land, buildings, furniture, equipments, inventories bank balance, intangible assets like patents and other legal rights and claims), Liabilities (what the institution owes to others, as for instance loans taken, other obligations that arise in the course of running the educational institutions), Equity (the net worth of the institution, calculated by subtracting liabilities from assets; it depicts the assets without the debts), income or revenues that enhance the value of the accounts say grants, fee, endowments, interest on the money deposited in banks, etc. and expenses that decreases the value of the accounts as for example through payment of salary, funds spent on maintenance of the campus, etc. Expenses decrease the equity unlike assets, which increase it.

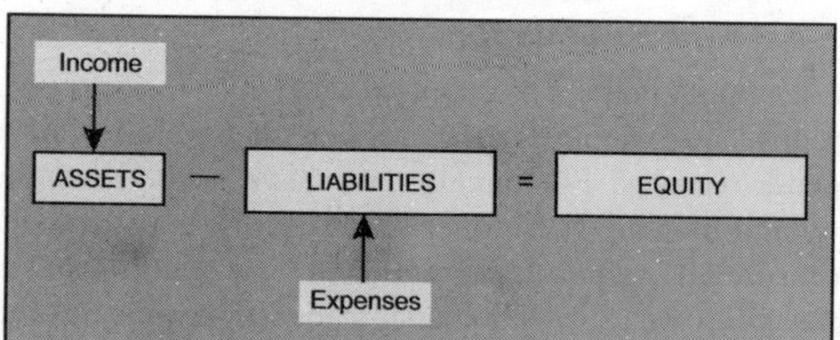

Figure 2.2: Interrelation among assets, liabilities, equity. Income and expenses

We may also infer that Assets–Liabilities=Equity+(Income–Expenses)

> **Example:** An educational institution's **assets** may be its savings, building, campus, equipments, books, etc. Its **liabilities** may be the loan it may have taken. The ***equity*** would be the difference between the values of assets and liabilities. The income is the fee, grants, endowments received. The **expenses** may be the salary, the rent (in case a building/equipments that has been rented), electricity, phone, etc.

Before we initiate further discussions on accounting, we shall introduce you to the basic concepts and conventions of accounting. You need to grasp these accounting principles so that you can follow the accounts maintained by the accountants working in your institution.

2.5 Concepts and Conventions in Accounting

Accounting is the language of business used by profit making as well as non profit making organizations to communicate financial information to the stakeholders. The language uses certain basic concepts and conventions with which you need to be familiar.

Some of the important concepts are as follows:

Entity Concept: Entity concept assumes that an organization, which for the purpose of this unit is an educational institution imparting higher education, has a distinct and separate entity from that of its owner(s). For the purposes of accounting, only those financial transactions that pertain to the educational institution are to be recorded in the books of accounts and not for the owners of the institution. This also holds good for proprietorships and partnerships, as the accounts for the business must be kept separate from those of the owners.

Example: When the owner invests money as capital into the educational institution, in accounting records, it is treated as liability of the educational institution to the owner. Similarly, when the owner withdraws any money from the educational institution, this is shown as a reduction in owner's capital and as a result liability of the educational institution also gets reduced by the same extent. Personal financial transactions of the owner/investor are not recorded in the books of accounts of educational institution unless it involves inflow or outflow of business funds. Entity concept thus avoids the mixing of the financial transactions of the organisation and that of its owner/investor.

Money Measurement Concept: Accounting involves recording of those transactions and events, which can be measured in terms of money. Only those transactions that can be expressed in monetary terms are recorded. For example, if a teacher is retiring, the amount payable to him/her towards gratuity, etc. will be recorded in the books of accounts. But the impact on the functioning of the institution due to his/her absence in terms of teaching may although be huge, it cannot be recorded in the books of accounts as this loss is not expressed in financial terms. This approach helps in having a common denominator, i.e. money for various expressions. This is important because it enables arithmetic operations like addition, subtraction, etc.

Cost Concept: Cost is the price (in monetary term) paid for goods and services at the time of acquiring them. According to cost concept, transactions are recorded in the books of accounts at the price paid, which in essence is the actual cost. For example if the educational institution purchases ten Personal Computers @ ₹ 35,000 each, further it spends ₹ 1000 towards transportation and ₹ 2000 for installation; the total amount/value at which these computers will be recorded in the books of accounts would be the sum of all these i.e. ₹ 3,53,000 (₹ 3,50,000+ 1,000 + 2,000). Suppose an educational institution purchases a piece of land, considered to be worth ₹ 10 lakhs, for ₹ 8 lakhs. This will be recorded in the books of accounts at the actual price paid for the purchase of land i.e. ₹ 8 lakhs.

Dual Aspect Concept: Dual aspect concept is also called Double Entry System. We shall explain it in the next section in detail. The key point is that all financial transactions have two dimensions. For example, if an organization has acquired an asset it must have resulted in one of the following events:

- Some other asset has been given up or
- The obligation to pay for it has arisen.

Example 1: If furniture worth ₹ 60,000 is purchased by an educational institution, on one hand the institution has acquired assets i.e. furniture, on the other hand either its bank balance will get reduced by ₹ 60,000 or liability will increase by the same amount.

Example 2: Mr. A starts an engineering college with investment of ₹ 100 Crores. There are two aspects of this transaction. In this transaction the college and Mr. A are separate entities. On one hand the College has acquired assets worth ₹ 100 Crores, while on the other hand the college, as a distinct entity, owes the same amount to Mr. A. Thus, this concept sets up the basic accounting equation: Assets = Liabilities + Capital (Owner's Equity).

Accrual Concept: According to this concept expenses incurred for a particular accounting period need to be reckoned in the same period, regardless of the fact whether these expenses have been paid in cash or not during that period. The same is the treatment for revenues i.e. incomes earned in a particular accounting period are construed as incomes of that period, regardless of the actual period of receipts.

Examples

(i) Fees due for the month of March 2011 are actually received in May 2011. It should be accounted as revenue for March 2011 although the amount was received in May 2011.

(ii) Electricity bill for the month of March 2011 of the Educational Institution was actually paid in the month of April 2011. This expense should be accounted in the financial year 2010-11 and not in 2011-12.

Accounting Period Concept: This concept requires that accounting reports should be prepared for a specified period, which is known as accounting period, in order to ascertain performance/results for reporting to the stakeholders. Conventionally, accounting period consists of a period of twelve months i.e. one year. Accounting period usually adopted by educational institutions is generally from April, 1 to March, 31 of a year. This is mainly to match the fiscal year of the government. The rationale for this concept is that it enables the assessment of the financial performance at periodic intervals and allows required remedial actions. However, accounting period can be of a period less than a year like half yearly basis, or for a quarter, etc.

The Going Concern Concept: According to this concept, it is assumed that the business will exist in the foreseeable future. For the purpose of an educational institution it could imply that the institution would exist for a long time to come and transactions are recorded on this basis. This concept forms the basis for undertaking expenditure that will provide benefit over a long period of time. It also helps in differentiating such expenditures from those with only short-term benefits.

Matching Concept: Requires that expenses recognized during an accounting period be matched with the revenue recognized in that period. It is the basis for detecting net income/profit of a form in a specific accounting period. When revenue exceeds expenses there is profit and vice versa (Khan & Jain, 2007). If revenues and related expenses be recorded in the same accounting period you can avoid overstatement of income in any one period.

Realization Concept: This is closely related to conservatism principle. It implies that revenue should be considered as earned/realized on the date of sales of goods/services to customers in consideration for cash/claims to cash and not on pending sales. In other words revenues are recognized only when they are earned or realized and cash or a claim to it is received. This is a conservatism which prevents the recording of money as soon as a contract is awarded.

Conventions regarding financial statements

There are certain conventions for accounting. We shall discus some of them.

Objectivity: As per this concept accounting will be recorded on the basis of objective evidence such as documents that state facts like invoices, receipts, bank statement and the like.

Consistency: This convention requires that same accounting procedures/practices should be used for preparing the financial statements for different periods. It facilitates comparison of financial performance of one period with another. The convention of consistency does not imply that no change should be made in accounting procedures. There should always be a scope for improvement but the justification for changes should be given in the statements. The impact of changes of procedures needs to be clearly stated. This will enable the users to analyze information in a more meaningful manner.

Disclosure: The convention of disclosure demands that all material facts and significant information should be disclosed in the financial statements. For example, in case of funds receivable from a particular source, not only the total amount receivable should be disclosed, but also the recovery of the amount, which may be doubtful, should be stated.

Conservatism: According to this convention, revenues are not anticipated, but provision is made for all known liabilities (expenses and losses) whether the amount of these is known with certainty or is at best only estimated. Basically, this convention does not encourage the anticipation or recognizing income when it is not certain. It advocates that any expenses/losses that can be reasonably ascertained should be taken into account. Financial statements are thus drawn on a conservative basis. It conveys that revenue, i.e. income is to be recognized for accounting purposes only when it is reasonably certain and recognize expenses as soon as they are undertaken. This avoids overstatement of the institutions' financial position and protects against inflated financial state. This brings in prudence in accounting procedures.

All these concepts and conventions are important but you will have to ensure that in your institution ethics underlie all accounting procedures. This implies that the accounting is done with figures that are accurate and complete and can be verified. Also, accounting is to be done in an objective manner without a conscious bias towards an individual/group.

2.6 Double Entry System: Classification of Accounts and Rules of Debit and Credit

Double Entry System

In the earlier section you have learnt about basic accounting concepts. We have also introduced you to the dual aspect concept of any financial transaction. We shall discuss yet another important aspect—Double Entry system. It is based on the dual aspect concept. This system recognises that each financial transaction has two aspects: a) receiving of a benefit/ value and b) giving the value. For this knowledge of classification of accounts and rules of debit and credit is required.

Classification of Accounts

Accounts help in systematically recording and tracking financial transactions. This is because an account is a summarized record of all transactions relating to a particular person, a thing or an item of income or expense. Every account has two sides for recording a transaction. The language of accounts uses the accounting terms; debit and credit to indicate the flow of money to or from an account. A debit means an entry on the left side of an account, and a credit means an entry on the right side of an account. We record an amount in the debit column, when it is being transferred to an account. We record an amount in the credit column, when it is being transferred from an account. But you need to remember that money always flows from the right column of one account to the left column of another account. You have read in double entry system that every change in the value of an account in the accounting equation must be balanced by a corresponding change in another, i.e. for each transaction, the total amount of money transferred from accounts must equal the total amount transferred to other accounts. Hence, in other words we may say that for every transaction, total debits must equal total credits. This is the main principle of accounting.

You need to balance both sides of the equation.

Debit indicates	Credit indicates
Increase in assets	Decrease in assets
Decrease in Liability	Increase in Liability
Decrease in Owners Equity	Increase in Owners Equity
Expenses/Losses	Income/Gains

Debits are assets/expense transactions; a debit transaction may be to reduce a credit balance or increase a debit balance).

Credits are from transaction leading to a financial liability or a gain; a credit transaction may be to lower a debit balance or increase a credit balance;

Debits ideally should equal credits of an organization at any particular point of time.

Financial transactions are classified into the following three categories:

Personal Accounts: It relates to persons e.g. debtors, creditors, etc.

Real Account: It relates to the assets of a firm or educational institution e.g. land, building, furniture, fittings, etc.

Nominal Accounts: It relates to expenses, losses, gains or income e.g. fees received from students, interest paid on loan, etc.

Rules of Debit and Credit

Let us now find out how duality aspect of a transaction is to be recorded, following the rules of debit and credit, in the books of accounts. These are as follows (Table 1):

Table 1

Nature of Account	Rule	Example
Personal account	Debit—the receiver Credit—the giver	Capital investment in the educational institution by owner/management (capital account) Loan from bank, financial institutions, etc.
Real account	Debit—what comes in Credit—what goes out	Land & building, Furniture, Computer etc.
Nominal Account	Debit—all losses & expenses Credit—all gains & income	Fees received (income) Electricity Charges (expense)

The rules described are explained with the help of following transactions:

Illustration

During the month of April 2010 an educational institution has made the following transactions:

Item No.	Date	Transactions
(1)	April 2	Owner invested a sum of ₹ 8,00,000
(2)	April 3	Purchased Office equipments worth ₹ 55,000 from 'S' Ltd.
(3)	April 5	Purchased laptops worth ₹ 1 lakh
(4)	April 15	Paid cash to printing press 'P' Ltd.—₹ 25,000
(5)	April 17	Received fees from students—₹ 70,000
(6)	April 18	Sold old car for ₹ 50,000
(7)	April 19	Paid salary of ₹ 3.00 lakhs

Analysis of transactions: The transactions carried out have been analysed in the following manner.

Item No 1. The institution received the amount from the owner. Cash is an asset, a real account. Cash comes in—Cash A/c is debited. The owner gives cash, owner is a personal account. Therefore, Capital (representing owner) account is credited.

Item No. 2: Office equipments i.e. assets (Real Account) come in as 'S' Ltd. sells them. Hence office equipments account (a/c) is to be debited and 'S' Ltd.'s a/c to be credited.

Item No. 3: Laptop (Real Account) comes in and cash (Real Account) goes out. Hence, Laptop a/c is to be debited and Cash a/c to be credited.

Item No. 4: Printing Charge being an expense is a nominal a/c, debit all expenses and losses and thus to be debited. Cash, a Real a/c goes out and hence to be credited.

Item No. 5: Cash i.e. asset (Real a/c) comes in and hence it is debited. Fees received from students being income is nominal account, credit all gains and income, hence Fees received a/c is credited.

Item No. 6: Old Car i.e. asset (real account) goes out. Hence, old Car a/c to be credited. Cash comes in, hence Cash a/c to be debited.

Item No.7: Salary being an expense (nominal a/c) to be debited. Cash (real a/c) goes out to be credited.

The accounting entries relating to above transactions are given below:

Item No.	Accounts Involved	Nature of A/c	Debit (₹)	Credit (₹)
1.	Cash	Real	800000	
	Capital	Personal		800000
2.	Office Equipments	Real	55000	
	S Ltd	Personal		55000
3.	Laptop	Real	100000	
	Cash	Real		100000
4.	Printing Charge	Nominal	25000	
	Cash	Real		25000
5.	Cash	Real	70000	
	Fees Received	Income		70000
6.	Cash	Real	50000	
	Old Car	Real		50000
7.	Salary	Nominal	300000	
	Cash	Real		300000

2.7 Accounting Cycle

The Accounting Process also known as the Accounting Cycle is sequence of activities that starts with financial transactions and ends with the closing of the books of accounts. Since this process is repeated in every accounting period, it is also termed as the accounting cycle. It involves the following major steps:

To identify transactions: Financial transactions carried out in the educational institution are required to be identified from the source document such as purchase order, invoice, receipt etc.

Example: Purchase of Office Equipments for the educational institution is a financial transaction. This can be identified, for recording in the books of accounts, from the source document bill/invoice issued by the supplier.

To determine transaction amount and identify accounts: For the purpose of recording transaction in the books of accounts it is necessary to determine the transaction amount and identify the accounts involved. You have already read about classification of accounts. It is important that financial transactions are properly classified and recorded in the books of accounts and that they are allocated to the correct heads of account.

To record transaction in the Journal: At this stage all the financial transactions are recorded by making entries in the journal book (it is also called day book) in chronological order on the basis of "Rules for Debit and Credit" as we have discussed. The narration about the transaction is given at foot of each entry. The journal is the entry point for financial transactions into the accounting system. Every transaction is accompanied by a description about it, the accounts affected, whether those accounts are increased/decreased and their extent as follows.

Journals

Date	Particulars	*LF	Amount (₹)	
			Debit	Credit
	Name of the a/c to be debited Name of the a/c to be credited (Narration about transaction in brief.)		√	√

LF: (Ledger Folio) i.e. Page No. of the Ledger

Date	Particular	LF	Amount (₹)	
			Dr.	Cr.
25/11/2010	Telephone charges		15,000	
	Cash a/c			15,000
	(Telephone charges paid for the month of November, 2010)			

Posting of Journal Entries to Ledger

Journal entries are then transferred to ledger accounts. Ledger is a book of account that contains record of all financial transactions in a summarised and classified form. It is also called the principal book of account since final information regarding the financial situation of an organization emerges from this book of accounts. The form of maintaining an account in the ledger is as follows.

Ledger

Debit (Dr.) Credit (Cr.)

Date	Particulars	*JF	Amount (₹)	Date	Particulars	JF	Amount (₹)
	To				By		

* JF: (Journal Folio) i.e. Page No. of the Journal

Illustration

Consider the following Journal Entry:

Date	Particulars	Ledger Folio	Amount (₹) Debit	Amount (₹) Credit
2011	Lab Equipments a/c		20,000	
March 25	To Bank a/c			20,000
	(Being Lab Equipments purchased)			

Lab Equipments a/c

Debit (Dr.) Credit (Cr.)

Date	Particulars	JF	Amount (₹)	Date	Particulars	JF	Amount (₹)
2011 March 25	To Bank a/c		20,000				

Bank A/c

Debit (Dr.) Credit (Cr.)

Date	Particulars	JF	Amount (₹)	Date	Particulars	JF	Amount (₹)
				2011 March 25	By Lab Equipments a/c		20,000

Balancing an account: Balancing is done at the end of a specific period—which may be week, month or year to ascertain the net of debit and credit amounts in an account. In order to ascertain the balance in any account at any given point of time one needs to total the two sides of an account and determine the difference. If the debit side is more than the credit side it will be a debit balance and vice versa. The debit balance is shown in the credit side as "Balance c/d" while the credit balance is shown in the debit side as "Balance c/d". Here 'c/d' stands for 'carried down'. It is imperative to mention that balancing is done only in respects of personal and real accounts, balances of which are shown in Balance Sheet. Balancing is not done in respects of nominal accounts as net of debit and credit is transferred to Income & Expenditure Account.

Preparing Trial Balance

The next step in accounting cycle is the preparation of the Trial Balance. This involves the listing of all the ledger accounts balances i.e. net of all debits and credits of ledger accounts.

Trial Balance is prepared at the end of a period that may be month, quarter, half year or the accounting period, usually the financial year.

Objectives of preparing Trial Balance

The objectives of preparing Trial Balance are to:

- ensure that the transactions recorded in the books of accounts have same debit and credit amount.
- ascertain the balance on any particular account in the ledger.
- ascertain that the balance of each ledger account has been computed correctly.
- facilitate the preparation of final accounts.
- ascertain that the balance of every ledger account has been transferred accurately and on the correct side of the trial balance.
- ascertain whether debit and credit sides of trial balance are in agreement, since it is a prima facie evidence of the arithmetical accuracy of the accounts books maintained.

However there are certain errors which are not detected by trial balance.

Errors not detected by Trial Balance

An agreed trial balance does not prove by itself that:

1. All transactions have been correctly analyzed and recorded in proper accounts. For example wages paid for installation of fixed asset might have wrongly been debited to wages account.
2. All the transactions have been recorded and nothing has been omitted.
3. Certain types of errors (listed below) remain undetected even after the preparation of trial balance.

Thus agreement of trial balance is not the conclusive proof of the accuracy of the books maintained.

Errors not revealed by (the preparation of) trial balance

Normally the following types of errors are not revealed by trial balance, despite agreement of debit and credit sides. Such errors (discussed in details in the Unit on Auditing) (ICWAI, 2003) are:

- Errors of omission: omission to record a transaction
- Posting of wrong amount on both the debit and credit sides of the account
- Errors of principle: when the accounting principle is disregarded in recording a transaction as for example, a capital item as revenue item and vice versa.
- Errors of duplication: Erroneously recording a transaction twice.
- Compensating Error: Errors made in posting of debit or credit entry compensated by an identical error of equal amount.

Let us now study the following illustration regarding Trial balance.

Illustrative Trial Balance
Trial Balance as on 31st March 2011

Account Head		L.F.	Debit Amount (₹)	Credit Amount (₹)
Cash			40,000	
Bank			1,50,000	
Buildings			16,00,000	
Vehicles			3,50,000	
Furniture & Fittings			2,00,000	
Accounts Receivable			55,000	
Inventories—Stationeries			15,000	
Accounts payable				60,000
Revenue				5,80,000
Capital				25,00,000
Interest—earned				1,10,000
Interest—expenses			50,000	
Wages & Salaries			5,00,000	
Electricity & Water Charges			30,000	
Depreciation—			2,60,000	
Buildings	2,00,000			
Vehicles	60,000			
			32,50,000	**32,50,000**

It is necessary to rectify the errors/discrepancies that might have occurred during the recording of transactions through adjustment in entries and posting them to the concerned ledger accounts.

Preparation of Financial Statements

The next step is to prepare financial statements. Unlike business organizations, financial statements of educational institutions comprise Income and Expenditure A/c and Balance Sheet.

The financial statements prepared in educational institutions are usually the following:

(i) Income and Expenditure account are prepared by taking into consideration all incomes, expenses, gains and losses.

(ii) Balance sheet is prepared with ledger balances of assets and liabilities.

Income and expenditure account

Educational institutions are considered to be non-profit seeking organizations. Hence, they may not prepare the profit and loss accounts. Instead they prepare the income and expenditure account to ascertain the operational result i.e. excess of income over expenditure and vice versa.

The income and expenditure account is prepared to ascertain:

- The actual income and expenses
- The operational surplus or deficit
- If there is balance between income and expenditure, etc.

A specimen of income and expenditure account is as follows:

Income and Expenditure Account
(For the year ended............)

Expenditure	Amount (₹)	Income	Amount (₹)
To Salaries and Wages		By Tuition Fees	
To Printing & Stationery		By Examination Fees	
To Telephone		By Interest on securities	
To Postage and Courier Charges		By Grants	
To Campus maintenance		By Conferences	

(Contd...)

Expenditure	Amount (₹)	Income	Amount (₹)
To Depreciation:			
• Land & building		By Income from renting of auditorium	
• Equipments		By Excess of expenditure over income (if deficit)	
• Furniture			
• Computer			
To News Papers & Journals			
To Advertisement			
To Honorarium			
To Excess of income over expenditure (if surplus)			

Preparation of Balance Sheet

Following the preparation of the income and expenditure account it is time to prepare a balance sheet. It shows the financial position of an organisation at the closing date of an accounting period. Balance sheet lists all the assets and liabilities such as capital fund, operational surplus/deficit, cash in hand, land & buildings, outstanding expenses, accrued income etc. Hence it is one of the most significant statements of assets, capitals and liabilities appearing in the books of accounts on a given date. It balances the assets against the liabilities (Rajendran, 2009).

A specimen of the balance sheet is as follows:

Balance sheet (as on ....)

Liabilities	Amount (₹)	Assets	Amount (₹)
Capital fund		Land and Buildings (Net of Depreciation)	
Add: Surplus		Furniture & Fixtures (Net of Depreciation)	
Less: Deficit		Equipments (Net of Depreciation)	
Endowment fund		Fixed deposits	
Donations		Inventories in hand	
Security Deposits		Bank	
Pre-received Income		Cash	
Outstanding expenses		Outstanding Income	
		Prepaid expenses	

The accounting cycle begins with journalizing the financial transactions, posting them to ledger, summarizing and balancing for preparing trial balance and finally it ends with preparation of financial statements at the close of accounting period. We shall now discuss the above aspect with the help of an illustration given below;

Illustration: On 1st March 2011 Mr. M started a Pvt. Educational Institution with ₹ 35,00,000 of which ₹ 10,00,000 were borrowed @ 12% p.a. from C bank. All the transactions have been carried out through bank.

Date	Transactions
March, 2011	
2	Hired a Building at a monthly rent of ₹ 55,000.
2	Purchased furniture and fittings worth ₹ 2,50,000.
3	Purchased Office equipments worth ₹ 75,000 from R.
4	Received ₹ 6,50,000 towards tuition fees.
28	Paid Electricity Charges for ₹ 25,000
29	Paid salaries for ₹ 5,00,000
30	Telephone Charges for ₹ 15,000
30	Interest of ₹ 10,000 paid to bank on loan (12% on ₹ 10 lacks= ₹ 120,000 Therefore, interest per month = 1,20,000/12 = ₹ 10,000).

Journal

Date	Particulars	L.F.	Dr. (₹)	Cr. (₹)
March 1 2011	Bank A/c Dr.		35,00,000	
	To Capital A/c			25,00,000
	To C Bank . A/c			10,00,000
	(Capital brought in and loan taken from C bank @ 12% p.a. to start an educational institution.)			
March 2	Rent A/c Dr.		55,000	
	To Bank A/c			55,000
	(Rent paid.)			
March 3	Furniture & Fittings A/c Dr.		2,50,000	
	To Bank A/c			2,50,000
	(Purchased furniture and fittings.)			
March 4	Office Equipments A/c Dr.		75,000	
	To 'R's A/c .			75,000
	(Office equipments purchased from R).			
March 5	Bank A/c Dr.		6,50,000	
	To Tuition Fee A/c			6,50,000
	(Received tuition fees.)			

Date	Particulars	L.F.	Dr. (₹)	Cr. (₹)
March 28	Electricity Charges A/c Dr. To Bank A/c (Electricity charges paid.)		25,000	25,000
March 29	Salaries A/c Dr. To Bank A/c (Paid salaries.)		5,00,000	5,00,000
March 30	Telephone Charges A/c Dr. To Bank A/c (Paid telephone charges.)		15,000	15,000
March 30	Interest A/c Dr. To Bank A/c (Interest paid on loan taken from bank .)		10,000	10,000
March 30	Income & Expenditure A/c Dr. To Rent A/c To Electricity Charges A/c To Salaries A/c To Telephone Charges A/c To Interest A/c (Transfer of expenses to Income and Expenditure A/c)		6,05,000	 55,000 25,000 5,00,000 15,000 10,000
March 30	Tuition fees A/c Dr. To Income of Expenditure A/c (Transfer of income to Income and Expenditure A/c)		6,50,000	6,50,000
March 30	Income & Expenditure A/c Dr. To Excess of Income Over Expenditure A/c (Being excess of income over expenditure)		45,000	45,000

Ledger

Capital A/c

Date	Particulars	J.F.	Dr. Amount (₹)	Date	Particulars	J.F.	Cr. Amount (₹)
2011				2011			
March 30	To Balance c/d*		25,00,000	March 1	By Bank A/c		25,00,000
			25,00,000				25,00,000
				April 1	By Balance b/d**		25,00,000
	*c/d = carried down,				** b/d = brought down		

C Bank (Loan) A/c

Date	Particulars	J.F.	Amount	Date	Particulars	J.F.	Amount
March. 30	To Balance c/d		10,00,000	March. 1	By Bank A/c		10,00,000
			10,00,000				10,00,000
				April 1	By Balance b/d		10,00,000

Rent A/c

Date	Particulars	J.F.	Dr. Amount (₹)	Date	Particulars	J.F.	Cr. Amount (₹)
2011				2011			
March. 2	To Bank A/c		55,000	March 30	By Income & Expenditure A/c		55,000
			55,000				55,000

Furniture & Fittings A/c

Date	Particulars	J.F.	Amount	Date	Particulars	J.F.	Amount
March 3	To Bank A/c		2,50,000	March 30	Balance c/d		2,50,000
			2,50,000				2,50,000
April 1	To Balance b/d		2,50,000				

Office Equipments A/c

Date	Particulars	J.F.	Amount	Date	Particulars	J.F.	Amount
March 4	To R A/c		75,000	March 30	Balance c/d		75,000
			75,000				75,000
April 1	To Balance b/d		75,000				

'R's A/c

Date	Particulars	J.F.	Amount	Date	Particulars	J.F.	Amount
March 30	To Balance c/d		75,000	March 4	By Office		75,000
			75,000		Equipments A/c		75,000
				April 1	By Balance b/d		75,000

Tuition Fees A/c

Date	Particulars	J.F.	Amount	Date	Particulars	J.F.	Amount
March 30	To Income & Expenditure A/c		6,50,000	March 5	By Bank A/c		6,50,000
			6,50,000				6,50,000

Electricity Charges A/c

Date	Particulars	J.F.	Amount	Date	Particulars	J.F.	Amount
March 28	To Bank A/c		25,000	March 30	By Income & Expenditure A/c		25,000
			25,000				25,000

Salaries A/c

Date	Particulars	J.F.	Amount	Date	Particulars	J.F.	Amount
March 29	To Bank A/c		5,00,000	March 30	By Income & Expenditure A/c		5,00,000
			5,00,000				5,00,000

Telephone Charges A/c

Date	Particulars	J.F.	Amount	Date	Particulars	J.F.	Amount
March 30	To Bank A/c		15,000	March 30	By Income & Expenditure A/c		15,000
			15,000				15,000

Interest A/c

Date	Particulars	J.F.	Amount	Date	Particulars	J.F.	Amount
March 30	To Bank A/c		10,000	March 30	By Income & Expenditure A/c		10,000
			10,000				10,000

Bank A/c

Date	Particulars	L.F.	Dr. Amount (₹)	Date	Particulars	L.F.	Cr. Amount (₹)
2011				2011			
March 1	To Capital A/c		25,00,000	March 1	By Furniture & Fittings A/c		2,50,000
	To C Bank A/c		10,00,000				
March 5	To Tuition fees A/c		6,50,000	March 2	By Rent A/c		55,000
				28	By Elect. Ch. A/c		25,000
				29	Salaries A/c		5,00,000
				30	Telephone Charges A/c		15,000
				30	Interest A/c		10,000
					By Balance c/d		32,95,000
			41,50,000				41,50,000
April 1	To Balance b/d		32,95,000				

Trial Balance
As at 31st March 2011

Particulars	Dr. Amount (₹)	Cr. Amount (₹)
Furniture & Fittings	2,50,000	
Equipments	75,000	
Balance at Bank	32,95,000	
Capital		25,00,000
C Bank (Loan taken)		10,00,000
R's A/c		75,000
Tuition Fees		6,50,000
Rent	55,000	
Electricity Charges	25,000	
Salaries	5,00,000	
Telephone Charges	15,000	
Interest on loan	10,000	
	42,25,000	**42,25,000**

Income & Expenditure A/c
For the month of March 2011

Expenditure	Dr. Amount	Income	Cr. Amount
To Rent	55,000	By Tuition Fees	6,50,000
Electricity Charges	25,000		
Salaries	5,00,000		
Telephone Ch.	15,000		
Interest on loan	10,000		
Excess of Income over Expenditure	45,000		
	6,50,000		**6,50,000**

Balance Sheet
As at 31st March 2011

Liabilities	Dr. Amount	Assets	Cr. Amount
Capital	25,00,000	Furniture & Fittings	2,50,000
		Office Equipments	75,000
Excess of Income over Expenditure	45,000	Balance at Bank	32,95,000
C Bank (Loan taken)	10,00,000		
R A/c (Amount payable against purchase of Equipments)	75,000		
	36,20,000		**36,20,000**

2.8 Capital and Revenue Transactions

A proper distinction between capital and revenue transactions is necessary for accounting of financial transactions of an educational institution. Both receipts and payments can be of capital or revenue nature. We shall now discuss how to distinguish or identify a financial transaction as capital or revenue.

Capital Transactions: It is generally of non-recurring nature. The financial transactions, which provide benefits or supply services to the organization, educational institution in the instant case, for more than one accounting period are considered as capital transactions. It is of two types—capital receipts and capital expenditure.

Capital receipts: It comprises amount invested in the educational institution for a long period, sale proceeds of fixed assets, long term loans from financial institution etc. Funding from sources that are usually received on a non-recurrent basis comprise such receipts.

Capital expenditure: It consists of expenditures, the benefits of which are carried over to several accounting periods, i.e. benefits of which are not exhausted in the accounting year of incurrence. It relates to expenses incurred for acquiring fixed assets e.g. buildings, laboratories, etc. It is of non-recurring nature. Both capital receipts and capital expenditures are shown in the Balance Sheet.

Revenue Transactions: The financial transactions, which provide benefits or supply services to an organization, educational institution in the instant case, for one accounting period only, are termed as revenue transactions. Revenue transactions can be Revenue Receipt or Revenue Expenditure.

Revenue receipts: Revenue earned in a recurring manner during the course of activities of an organization. In an educational institution it constitutes of tuition fees, annual fees, income from investments, other miscellaneous receipts, etc.

Revenue expenditure: Expenditure which yields benefits only for one accounting period is called revenue expenditure. It is usually of recurring nature. It is incurred to carry out the routine activities of an organization. It consists of salaries, electricity charges, telephone charges, consumables for laboratories, maintenance of building, etc.

2.9 Books of Account/Accounting Records

We shall now discuss the various accounting records/books of accounts to be maintained by an educational institution. The managers of educational institution need to ensure the proper maintenance of the books of accounts, on day-to-day basis in a chronological manner. Following accounts/registers/records are usually maintained by an educational intuition:

Journal or Day books to record financial transactions in chronological order. Various types of day books are Purchase day Book, Sales day Book, Purchase Return or Sales return Book etc. for recording financial transaction relating to credit purchase/sale and return thereof.

Journal proper is for recording financial transactions that cannot be recorded in the above mentioned day-books or Cash/ Bank book. It contains journal entries relating to opening/ closing entries, transfer entries, adjustment entries, rectification entries and miscellaneous other entries like credit purchases/ sales of fixed assets, investments, loss by theft/accident, fire etc.

Fees Receipt books with all the pages serially numbered so as to trace out lost and damaged pages.

Cash book/Bank book to record financial transactions made in cash or through bank. The Cash/Bank book should be balanced daily so that cash received on a day is balanced against the amount spent on the same day. Details of cheques received/paid as a day's income and expenses also need to be entered in this book of account. It should be signed by the controlling officer at the end of each day.

Ledger is called the principal book of account. It contains records of financial transaction in classified and summarised form. It is the head-wise repository of all transactions. It is to be maintained because the accounts of an educational institution are required to be maintained under the double entry system. There are different types of ledgers as general ledger, fees ledger, credit ledger, etc.

- General Ledger: It is a book with all major items of the budget with few pages for each item and daily expenses on each item is recorded therein. All information in receipt books, vouchers and cash books enter the ledger making it comprehensive.
- Fees Ledger: To record all information pertaining to student's fees, their date of receipt, amount received, outstanding balance, etc.
- Creditor's Ledger: It is a book with the list of creditors, the amounts owed to the institution by each, dates of settlement, outstanding amounts, etc. Updating the entries regularly is necessary to keep track of creditors.

Fixed Assets Register: It is a register pertaining to fixed assets like land, buildings, etc.

Stores Ledger: It is a record where stationery and other inventories are listed by following perpetual inventory system (balancing after every receipt/issue of an item) to keep track of the institution's inventories.

Fee Register: Register showing fees that are recoverable and recovered.

Fee concession register

Student's Security deposit registers

Register for recording the donations received

Log book for staff car and other vehicles of the educational institution.

Voucher files month-wise to detail the purpose of the payment, its date, amount, the budgetary items within which the expense is being incurred, authority sanctioning the payment, etc. The voucher should be written and signed before money is released. It must bear a number that can be quoted. Receipts obtained following purchases should be attached to the voucher. It thus informs about the expense incurred.

Monthly Bank Reconciliation Statements

Above list of books of accounts is not an exhaustive one and you may need additional records depending upon the activities of the educational institution.

2.10 Final Accounts of Educational Institutions

The objective of educational institution is to provide education, a kind of welfare service to the society. Educational institutions are supposed to be non-profit seeking organizations. Hence, they do not prepare Profit and Loss Account. However, educational institutions need to keep track of their income and expenditure, exercise control over utilization of funds, to ascertain whether their earnings are sufficient to meet expenses and financial position at end of the accounting period. The final accounts of an educational institution, which is a 'non-profit-seeking organisation', comprise the following:

(i) Receipts and Payments Account

(ii) Income and Expenditure Account, and

(iii) Balance Sheet.

Receipts And Payments Account: It is a summary of all receipts and payments made in cash or through bank. Receipts and payments of both capital and revenue nature are shown in this statement irrespective of the accounting period that the financial transactions pertain to i.e. previous period, current or next accounting period. The opening balance shown on the receipts side of Receipts and Payments account indicates cash in hand/cash at bank at the beginning of the accounting period and the closing balance shown on the payments side of this account represents cash in hand and bank balance as at the end of the accounting period. If the payment side exceeds receipt side it represents bank overdraft. An illustrative Receipts and Payments Account is given below:

Receipt and Payment Account for the year ending March 31, 2011

Dr. **Cr.**

Receipts		Amount ₹	Payments	Amount ₹
1.4.2010				
Cash in hand		25,000	Salaries and wages	90,000
Cash at Bank		30,000	Electricity Charges	25,000
Students' Fees			Telephone Charges	10,000
2006-07	25,000		Printing of Learning Material	30,000
2007-08	2,00,000		Stationeries	7,000
2008-09	50,000	2,75,000		
			Investments	3,50,000
Governments Grants		3,00,000	31.3.2011	
Interest on Investments		20,000	Cash in hand	68,000
Sale of Learning Material		30,000	Cash at Bank	1,00,000
		6,80,000		6,80,000

Income and Expenditure Account: Income and Expenditure are similar to Profit and Loss Account. All revenue income/ earnings and revenue expenses pertaining to the current accounting period are placed in the account to ascertain operating performance i.e. surplus or deficit. Excess of income over expenses is surplus and excess of expenses over income is deficit.

Difference between receipts and payments account and income and expenditure account stands as follows:

Basis of difference	Receipt and Payment A/c	Income and Expenditure A/c
Nature	Summary of Cash & Bank Book	Similar to Profit & Loss A/c
Items considered	Both capital and revenue income and expenses	Only revenue income and revenue expenses
Period	Irrespective of the accounting period i.e. receipts/payments may relate to previous, current or succeeding accounting period	Expenses & income of current accounting period considered

(Contd...)

Basis of difference	Receipt and Payment A/c	Income and Expenditure A/c
Debit side	All receipts	All expenses and losses
Credit side	All payments	All income and gains
Nature of transaction	Only cash transaction	Both cash and credit transactions
Opening Balance	Cash in Hand/at bank or bank overdraft at the beginning of accounting period	None
Closing Balance	Cash in Hand/at bank or bank overdraft at the closing date of accounting period	Debit balance represents deficit, Credit balance indicates surplus

Balance sheet: It is prepared to ascertain financial position. Assets are shown on the right side and liabilities on the left side of the Balance Sheet. On the liabilities side, there will be Capital Fund or General Fund in place of Capital. Excess of income over expenditure is added to it, while deficit i.e. excess of expenses over income is deducted from this fund.

2.11 Use of Computers in Accounting

Now you know that accounting involves an elaborate process, which in modern educational institutions with a variety of transactions and complexities may be a time consuming and laborious process. Therefore, computers are used for data storing, processing and sharing. Specially designed soft wares are available that can take care of the accounting of an institution. A computerised accounting system is actually an accounting information system that processes the financial transactions and events as per Generally Accepted Accounting Principles (GAAP) to provide reports as and when needed. They are based on database, implemented using a database management system. The accounting database has an active interface that uses accounting application programs and reporting system. They can help in online input and storage of accounting data. There is logical scheme for codification of accounts and transactions as every account and transaction is assigned a unique code and there is grouping of accounts from the very beginning. One can also get reports instantly like Stock Statement, Trial Balance, Balance Sheet, Returns, etc. The accounting packages may be ready to use type or customised type or

Tailored. Depending upon the need of the organisation they are selected.

While choosing software you have to consider factors such as the volume of transactions in your institution, the soft ware's cost effectiveness and flexibility in terms of data entry, demands of reports, operating systems and hardware. Moreover it should be easy to upgrade and alter, require less maintenance, be user friendly, provide security, prevent unauthorised access, allow efficient data transfer. You may also consider the reputation and after sales support provided by the vendor.

2.12 Summary

Irrespective of the nature of an organization i.e. whether it is a business organization or a non-trading concern like an educational institution, recording of day-to-day financial transactions is essential. This is mainly because such a practice helps to track the inflow and outflow of funds on a daily basis and ascertain the financial position of the institution on a particular date. However, recording the financial transactions has to be a systematic process and follow the generally accepted principles and guidelines for accounting. While, bookkeeping involves regularly recording in financial terms all financial transactions carried out by an organization according to certain rules and with certain objectives, accounting involves recording, verifying, classifying, summarizing and reporting information in terms of money, transactions and events, which are financial in nature. The scope of accounting is thus wider than book-keeping. Accounting is based on certain concepts like the entity concept, money measurement concept, cost concept etc. and conventions such as consistency, conservatism, disclosure, etc. Double entry system of accounting recognises that each financial transaction has two aspects; a) receiving of a benefit/value and b) giving the value. For this, knowledge of classification of accounts and rules of debit and credit are required, which have been discussed at length in this chapter along with discussions on analysis of a transaction as per the established rules of debit and credit.

There are various stages of an accounting process. The first step is to identify the transaction. To determine transaction amount and identify the accounts is the next step. This is followed by recording the transaction in the journal, posting the journal entries to ledger, preparing trial balance and preparing final accounts and financial statements. Educational institutions are considered to be non-profit seeking organizations. Hence they may not prepare the profit and loss accounts. Instead they prepare the income and expenditure account to determine the surplus and the deficit situation. Thereafter, balance sheet is prepared.

A proper distinction between capital and revenue transactions is necessary for accounting of financial transactions of an educational institution. Capital Transactions are generally of non-recurring nature. Revenue Transactions are the financial transactions, which provide benefits or supply services to an organization, educational institution in the instant case, for one accounting period only. The managers of educational institution need to ensure the proper maintenance of the books of accounts, on day-to-day basis in a chronological manner.

The various accounting records/books of accounts are journal, fee receipt book, cash book etc., which are to be maintained by the educational institution. The final accounts of an educational intuition, which is a 'non-profit-seeking organisation', comprise—Receipts and Payments Account, Income and Expenditure Account, and Balance Sheet. All these activities are done efficiently if computers and special soft wares available for accounting are used.

2.13 Self Assessment

2.13.1 *Questions*

Answer the following questions:

(1) Give any three reasons why your institution should maintain accounts systematically.

(2) In a private college, from the accounts, the owner withdraws ₹ 1,50,000 for his personal use. How will the institution account for such a transaction?

(3) Telephone bill for the month of January 2011 was paid in the month of April 2011. This expense should be accounted in which financial year?

(4) List the financial records maintained.

(5) What are the advantages of using computers in accounting?

2.13.2 *Clues*

(1)

- To record all financial transactions on a permanent basis
- To enable to prepare income & expenditure account at the end of accounting period
- To prepare Balance Sheet on a particular date

(2) Withdrawal of money, which the owner has invested in the college as capital, would be recorded as withdrawal in the books of accounts. However, if the owner spends from his own source of fund for his family, such transaction will not be recorded in the books of accounts of the college because it has no effect on the financial status of the institution, which is a separate entity.

(3) The financial year 2010-11 (Accrual Concept)

(4) Various day books, cashbook, ledger, etc.

(5) Computers can help in online input and storage of accounting data. There is logical scheme for codification of accounts and transactions as every account and transaction is assigned a unique code and there is grouping of accounts from the very beginning. One can also get reports instantly like Stock Statement, Trial Balance, Balance Sheet, Returns, etc.

2.14 Activities

You may carry out these activities for gaining a better understanding of this chapter.

1. Visit an educational institution and interview the personnel manning the finance department about the users of financial statements.

2. For electricity bill paid and equipments purchased by an educational institution during a financial year, study how accounts have been maintained.

3. Prepare a trial balance for an institution with data collected on any 7 transactions.

4. List the books of accounts maintained by a school and an institution imparting higher education.

References

Bose, S. & Agarwal, N. (2007). Maintaining school accounts. *School governance and financial management*. PG Diploma in School Leadership and Management. New Delhi: IGNOU.

Gupta, S.P. (2004). *Management Accounting*. Agra: Sahitya Bhawan Publication.

ICWAI, (2003). Study Notes-*Financial Accounting Fundamentals*. Directorate of Studies, Kolkata.

Khan, M.Y. & Jain, P.K. (2007). *Management Accounting*. 4thEdition. New Delhi: Tata McGraw Hill.

Rajendran, G. (2009). *Management Accounting*. New Delhi: Regal Publishers

Shukla, S.M. (2004). *Bookkeeping and Accountancy*. Agra: Sahitya Bhawan Publication.

Websites

You may also read the content given in the following Websites (websites may not be permanent).

http://www.netmba.com/accounting/fin/process/Retrieved on 26/12/08.

http://www.gnucash.org/docs/v1.8/C/gnucash-guide/basics_accounting1.html Retrieved on 20/9/10.

http://basiccollegeaccounting.com/going-concern-concept/Retrieved on 20/9/10.

http://www.bized.co.uk/learn/accounting/infosystems/bait/work06.htm Retrieved on 20/9/10. http://www.futureaccountant.com/accounting-process/study-notes/financial-accounting-account-types.php Retrieved on 20/9/10

Auditing

3

3.1 Introduction

In the earlier chapter you have been introduced to the concept of accounting. This chapter will give you an idea of another important financial activity—auditing. You may be wondering why discussion on auditing has been included in this chapter as auditing would be done mainly by an external agency with the necessary expertise. However, the auditor(s) will apply certain techniques and methods for collection of evidences and carrying out examination. As a manager you need to be aware of these activities so that you can co-ordinate and respond to the requirements of the external auditor.

Auditing in general means thorough and careful examination, inspection and like. In the context of an educational institution and its financial management, it mainly refers to the examination of financial accounts. As you read this chapter, you will come across, discussions on important aspects related to auditing like the concept of auditing and its importance, the techniques of auditing, internal auditing, audit programme and audit report.

3.2 Objectives

Following a study of this chapter, you are expected to:

- describe the concept of auditing;
- discuss the stages of auditing;
- describe the various techniques of auditing;
- explain the importance of internal auditing; and
- discuss the requirements of an audit program.

3.3 What is Auditing?

Auditing basically refers to a process involving comprehensive evaluation of something, which can be personal qualities, process, project or product. There can be different types of auditing such as educational audit, environmental audit, performance audit and so on. However for the purpose of this chapter, we shall restrict the scope of auditing to the financial matters of educational institutions. Audit is not something new. Earlier the owners of business houses hired as and when they felt it necessary, those with expertise in checking the books of accounts. This was an informal practice resorted to more for detecting fraud and misappropriations rather than for statutory compliance. Later on with industrialization and involvement of several stakeholders in the functioning of an organization, the need for generally accepted methods of accounting and regular auditing emerged.

For many of us, the term auditing is not new. But what does it actually mean? The commonly held perception of auditing is to detect the veracity of the accounts maintained. With an overt emphasis on detection of errors and financial embezzlement, it is often considered to be an activity akin to policing. But today there is a more comprehensive view as to the objectives of auditing. Auditing can be defined as a process of collection and evaluation of evidence for the purpose of reporting on economic information (Gupta and Arora, 1996). The three components of this definition have been explained as follows:

Economic information may include:

- Financial statements such as balance sheet, profit and loss account, income and expenditure, etc.
- Costing statements like cost sheet, variance analysis statement, etc.
- Statements prepared to facilitate managerial control such as statements showing actual performance vis a vis targets.

Collection and evaluation of evidence: Auditors study the economic information, collect and evaluate evidences on the basis of which reporting is done.

Reporting: The purpose of auditing is basically reporting about the economic information. The auditor examines the information being audited and prepares a written report.

Auditing is thus a periodic, systematic and independent examination of financial systems and financial information like accounts, tax returns, and other financial and relevant records of the organisation. In other words it takes stock of the assets and the liabilities, the financial transactions and controls as well as the compliance of the institution with some set of standards, policies, rules, etc. that govern financial management of the institution. It thus gives a comprehensive picture of the financial situation of the organisation. It is a formal activity and leads to the expression of an opinion in a formal manner by the auditor regarding the aspects audited.

Audit is an instrument of financial control. It acts as a safeguard on behalf of the proprietor(s) (government/funding agency) against extravagance, carelessness or fraud on the part of the proprietors' agents or servants in the realization and utilization of the funds or other assets. An audit also ensures that the accounts maintained truly represent facts and that expenditure has been incurred with due regularity and propriety. All these are done with the help of experts called 'auditors' (ICWAI, 2002).

Audit can be of different types such as:

- Independent financial audit: An audit by an outside agency or individual(s) not connected with the organization being audited. This is also known as external/statutory audit.
- Internal audit: It is an audit carried out by the employees of an organization to ensure that the procedures, operations, and accounting practices of the organisation are being carried out properly as per the established practices and rules of the institution. We shall discuss it later in this chapter.
- Compliance audit: It may be carried out by a regulatory agency exclusively to assess compliance with established policies, rules and regulations, i.e. to check whether the

organisation adheres to generally accepted standards set by the governing bodies.

Is auditing same as investigating? No, it is not. While the latter follows a suspicion as to a wrong doing, the former is a routine affair with fraud detection being incidental. An auditor is not supposed to be a detective or approach his/her work with suspicion or with forgone conclusions or prejudices. S/he is a watchdog but not a bloodhound (Obiter dicta of Lord Justice Lopes quoted by Tandon, 1978).

3.3.1 *Objectives of auditing*

The main objective of auditing an educational institution is to ascertain that the financial statements of the institution reflect a true and fair view of the financial position and working results at the end of an accounting period. As mentioned earlier, it aims to collect and evaluate audit evidence to form and communicate to the users of the financial statements, an audit opinion, expressed as a formal report. The report is a reflection of the reliability and hence, the credibility of the financial assertions of the organization. Audit is thus an instrument of financial control. It determines the fairness with which an organisation has presented its financial statements and acts as a safeguard for the stakeholders against extravagance, carelessness or fraud in financial matters such as realization and utilization of the funds or other assets.

An audit checks that the expenditure has been incurred with due regularity and propriety. It also helps in determining whether the generally accepted accounting principles have been adhered to. Apart from the arithmetical accuracy of the books of accounts, the veracity of the records of the transactions that have been entered is also checked by scrutinizing the vouchers, pay orders, and other documents supporting the records maintained. Auditing may also check the compliance, i.e. whether the institution is complying with the financial policies, rules and regulations pertaining to tax, levies, income, spending, investing, borrowing, etc.

As mentioned earlier, detection of errors and fraud is not the primary objective of auditing but is incidental to the main objective of auditing. We may hold a general assumption that errors are generally unintentional. However, the possibility of fraudulent intentions leading to mistakes/errors cannot be ruled out. The discrepancy in the accounts may be attributed to human error or fraud. Let us discuss some of the common types of errors. You have studied in the earlier unit that the total of credit and debit balances must match each other or else error(s) can be assumed to be leading to the disagreement in the figures. However not all sorts of errors are reflected in the trial balance. Auditing may disclose these errors. Errors of accounting procedure can be classified into the following types:

- *Errors of Principle*: Such errors occur when transactions are not recorded according to the fundamental principles of accounting. For example, revenue expenditure is treated as capital expenditure or vice versa. Such errors may affect the balance sheet.
- *Clerical Errors*: Clerical errors are usually of two types:
  1. Errors of omission: These errors occur when transactions are not recorded in the book of accounts either wholly or partially. For example scrutiny of fees account may reflect that fees received has been accounted for 11 months as against 12 months. It may be due to omission in entering a transaction in the books of original entry or due to omission in posting a transaction from the books of original entry to the account concerned in the ledger. This type of error does not affect agreement of trial balance and the omission may remain undetected.
  2. Errors of commission: When a transaction is incorrectly recorded as for e.g. if purchase invoice of ₹1800 is entered as ₹ 8100, there is an error of commission. Errors of commissions may be due to reasons like incorrect posting, errors in calculation, balancing, etc. Non-agreement of the trial balance can detect some of them.
- *Compensating errors*: When an error is counter-balanced by another error in such a way that it is not disclosed by

the trial balance, such an error is called compensating error. For example, a cash sale of ₹ 2000 has been recorded in the cashbook as ₹ 200, while another cash sale of ₹ 200 has been recorded as ₹ 2000.

- *Errors of Duplication*: When an entry in a book of original entry is made twice and is also posted twice, errors of this type are made.
- *Detection and Prevention of Fraud*: Auditing intends to detect, correct as well as prevent fraud. However, fraud cannot be totally eliminated. Evidences such as records that are missing/destroyed/manipulated/tampered/counterfeit point to fraud rather than error. In such cases managers of the institution may have to get the matter investigated.

Fraud means an act of deception or cheating in order to get a financial gain. Fraud may pertain to the aspects such as the following:

- *Embezzlement of Cash*: Misappropriation of cash is a very common problem. Cash may be misappropriated in a number of ways such as: omitting entry of cash received or entering amounts lesser than that received, making fictitious entries or an amount greater than actual ones on the payment side of the cashbook.
- *Falsification of accounts*: This is done with a view to suppress the true picture of the financial position by showing fictitious income or expenses, under or over valuation of assets and liabilities, etc.
- *Misappropriation of goods*: Fraud may also take place through misappropriation of goods. Maintenance of proper records of inventories, physical verification, etc. may help in avoiding this type of fraud.

Managers of an educational institution should see that unscrupulous employees do not resort to such malpractices as their detection during auditing may make the managers answerable.

We can now summarize the advantages of audit as:

- Audit gives a clear picture of the financial health of an organization at a certain point of time and this picture is necessary for the efficient financial management of the organization itself and may also be required by the stakeholders.
- Audit helps to detect and prevent errors and frauds.
- Auditing enhances accuracy, authenticity and reliability in the maintenance of the books of accounts and financial statements.
- Regular audit of accounts of the educational institution keeps the accounts staff careful and vigilant and keep information up to date.
- Government authorities including Income Tax departments generally accept the income and expenditure accounts and balance sheets that are duly audited by a qualified auditor. Thus audit gives wider acceptability to the financial records of the institution.
- Audited accounts are needed if funds are to be borrowed from financial institutions, in settlement of insurance claims and other legal matters.
- Audited financial statements may be very useful in comparing financial performance of the institution with that of the previous year(s).
- The auditor may give suggestions for better compliance including systemic improvements and modifications in the accounts and internal controls. On technical points the educational institution head may even seek the advice of the auditors.

You will now agree that as mentioned earlier, audit is a tool for efficient financial management. The auditor may require any information or explanation from the competent authority of an educational institution. It is obligatory on the part of the competent authority to furnish any such information as required by the auditor. The managers of educational institutions should facilitate the auditor to perform his/her duty by providing access and allowing the examination of the books of accounts, financial statements, vouchers and other documents, physical verification and inspection of assets, etc. as may be necessary for the purpose of audit report (Commonwealth Secretariat, 1993).

3.3.2 *Stages involved*

There are different stages in an audit engagement. Each stage involves critical decisions on the part of the auditor. The stages are the following:

- **Accept/reject decision:** At the outset the auditor conducts preliminary inquiry about the client's activities i.e. various activities of the educational institution in the instant case, in order to arrive at a decision on the acceptance or rejection of an audit proposal of the educational institution.
- **Audit planning:** Once the auditor accepts the audit work, the next step is to prepare an audit plan. Here the auditor decides about appropriate audit approach for conducting the audit. The auditor tries to understand the nature of the organization and its major activities and also the environment in which it operates and then decides to carry out audit in the institution.
- **Evaluation of internal control procedure:** In order to decide on the reliance to be placed on one or more control procedures of the client organization vis-a vis extent of verification/checking required, the auditor evaluates the effectiveness of the control mechanisms in vogue. The auditor then decides whether the internal control system of the client organization can be relied upon. If internal controls are found to be strong, this will lessen the amount of 'substantive' work the auditor needs to do. But in some cases an auditor may not depend upon internal controls and carries out substantive auditing. If internal controls are considered to be strong, auditors may rely more on Substantive Analytical Procedures (comparing financial data with non-financial data, to check the figures and the investigation of

deviations and relationships that are inconsistent with other relevant or expected information by a significant amount). If internal controls are perceived to be weak, auditors may rely more on Substantive Tests of Details (testing account balances to check their correctness or selecting a sample of items from the major account balances, and finding evidence, e.g. Invoices, bank statements for the items sampled, etc.).

- **Substantive testing:** At this stage, the auditor carries out vouching and verification of books of accounts, documents and records in order to gather substantive evidence (i.e. evidence as to the completeness, propriety and accuracy of the various monetary transactions, records maintained, etc.) for the purpose of determining the extent of true and fair view of the financial statements made by the organisation.
- **Forming an Opinion and Reporting:** Finally, on the basis of the evaluation of internal controls, vouching and verification of books of accounts and records, the auditor forms an opinion about the veracity of the financial statements and the overall financial picture depicted. The auditor then prepares a report. The report includes important matters that came to the auditor's attention during auditing. It is also ensured by the auditor that adequate and relevant evidences are there for any assertion. The evidences therefore are evaluated and reviewed before a report is prepared on their basis.

3.3.3 *Whom to have as auditor?*

Educational institutions usually engage auditors through the terms of a formal contract, which is binding for both parties. The contract with the auditor must clearly spell out the terms of reference, remuneration payable and time period by which audit work has to be completed and report is to be submitted. Auditor should be appointed by the governing body of the educational institution.

The qualities expected of an auditor whom an educational institution could entrust with the task of auditing are as follows:

- First of all an auditor should possess sound knowledge in the fundamental principles and theories of accounting, auditing, taxation, etc.
- S/he should possess the necessary qualifications. Preferably, an auditor should be a professionally qualified accountant.
- The auditor should also have sufficient knowledge of the laws, statutes and provisions applicable to the organization and the client's nature of activities and its peculiar features.
- An auditor should also possess certain personal attributes such as, tactfulness, cautious approach, firmness, analytical ability, trustworthiness, patience, etc.
- Most importantly, s/he needs to have the highest degree of integrity.
- An Auditor should not be influenced by those with vested interests while conducting the audit.

3.4 Techniques of Auditing

You now know that auditing aims to gather evidences about the financial information provided by the organization. The evidence collected should ideally be adequate, useful, relevant and persuasive. The evidence also has to be logically related to the audit objectives. The evidence may be of analytical type that describes the relationships among variables. It may also be documentary or may be physically obtained through observation or it could be testimonial i.e. statements made by concerned people and corroborated.

Various techniques may be used for collecting data for evidence during auditing. The techniques are not static and auditor may have to change the auditing techniques in order to keep pace with developments in the system of maintaining accounts such as computerization, disclosure norms, growing organizational complexities, etc. Some of the techniques usually adopted by the auditors are as follows:

Determining the accuracy of arithmetical calculations: This is done by checking the process of calculations made in the books of accounts i.e. totaling, carrying forward, balancing or posting to a ledger or financial statements or by recompilation of figures. This is a very simple technique to judge arithmetical accuracy.

Vouching: A voucher is any document supporting a transaction. Vouching is the process of establishing accuracy and authenticity of entries in accounts, funds, or other records. It involves examination of entries in the books of accounts with reference to supporting evidence of the transactions such as invoices, receipts, paid checks or other original documents. The auditor also needs to examine the aspects relating to authorization and propriety of financial transactions, assess the appropriateness of the accounting treatment of the transactions.

Physical examination and count: It is also known as physical verification or inspection. The auditor may carry this out in order to verify tangible assets of the educational institution. Physical examination may include identification, counting (assessing) and to a certain extent evaluation of the quality of the items represented in the accounts.

Examination of documents and comparing them with records/books of accounts: Documentary evidences may be examined to verify their appropriateness i.e. legitimacy of transaction, authenticity, i.e. genuineness of the document, authorization i.e. whether the evidence contains the necessary approval of the signing authority.

Confirmation: This is a process of ascertaining the authenticity and accuracy of the information available in the books of accounts and financial statements by direct communication with the party to a transaction. The auditor obtains written statements and certificates from independent parties regarding certain transactions.

Retracing bookkeeping procedures: Postings from the books of prime entry are traced to ledgers or fresh trial balances of various ledgers prepared. The auditor thus repeats a number of bookkeeping procedures.

Inquiry: An auditor inquires in order to collect evidence of the operation of internal controls, ascertain terms and conditions of certain transactions. Usually, the auditor conducts inquiry through predetermined questionnaires.

Scanning: An account or a book of original entry is scanned to find out whether the transaction follows a logical pattern or something is unusual.

Flow Charting: Auditors may prepare and use flow charts that depict graphically the various activities, controls and stages of the system, to analyse the system and evaluate its effectiveness.

Reconciliation and account analysis: The technique of reconciliation is basic to all auditing. An auditor may have to carry out reconciliation of a number of accounting figures such as bank accounts, fees receipts, expenditures, inventories, etc. The auditor may also resort to analyzing financial statements. Analytical procedures consist of the analysis of significant ratios and trends including the resulting investigation of fluctuations and relationships that are inconsistent with other relevant information or deviate from predicted amounts. By using analytical procedures, the auditor may detect circumstances that call into question the appropriateness of the transactions.

Current techniques of auditing also include risk assessment, materiality (relative significance of a matter in the context of the whole financial statements such as the significance of an omission on the auditor's report), analytical review, etc.

3.5 Internal Control: Internal Audit and Internal Check

You have read that auditing is carried out by an independent agency (not connected with the educational institution) having professional expertise in the field of finance and accounts. This kind of auditing is also known as external auditing or statutory auditing (if required by the statute governing educational institution). However, educational institutions like any other organization also need to exercise Internal Control. Internal control is a means by which an educational institution directs and monitors its resources through its internal mechanisms. It aims to bring about efficiency of operations and thus leads to the attainment of the organizational goals. It also safeguards resources and brings about reliability in financial reporting. It helps in preventing and detecting misappropriation of financial resources and assets. The assets could be physical i.e. tangible as well as intangible like reputation, fame, etc. Thus it ensures correct financial statements and compliance with policies and regulations. It is depicted through Figure 3.1.

- Whole set of controls → Financial / Non-financial
- Established by the management
- With a view to:
    - Carry on functions/activities in an orderly manner
    - Protect assets
    - Ensure accuracy and reliability of records
    - Promote operational efficiency
    - Ensure compliance with policies, rules and regulations,

Figure 3.1: Internal Control

Internal control in educational institutions is for ascertaining aspects such as the following:

- Propriety of transactions
- Reliability, accuracy and complete information
- Compliance with established policies, statutes and rules of the government and the educational institution.
- Ascertaining the safety of assets of the organization for instance checking to find out if anyone can have free access to items that are supposed to be guarded.
- Ascertaining if the operations of the institutions are economic and efficient.

Thus, internal control is a tool to ensure smooth and economic functioning of the institution. Internal controls are exercised either by *preventive measures* (to stop an unwanted outcome before it happens) or by *feedback* (to find out about the problem and act before it grows).

How is Internal Control brought about? Some of the means of internal control are the following:

Internal check: It is an arrangement of staff duties whereby no one person is allowed to carry out and record every aspect of a transaction. This ensures that without collusion between two or more persons, fraud is prevented and at the same time, the possibilities of errors are also reduced to a minimum. Internal checks make misappropriation of cash and other assets and subsequently covering it up by entering corresponding amounts in the accounts difficult. Physical controls are also used like gates, locks, security guards, etc. that deny direct access to assets. Besides, errors are also checked and rechecked and hence they are more likely to be noticed and rectified. Internal check system thus aims to:

- Specifically identify the person responsible for a particular act, error, default, omission, etc., and thus helps in fixing responsibilities.
- Confirm facts and entries from multiple sources by creation and preservation of necessary records.
- Minimize bottlenecks and establish an even flow of work.
- Reduce the chances of frauds, theft or irregularities.

Thus, under internal check system:

- No one person is authorized to carry out all the operations involved in a transaction.
- System institutes cross checks and cross reconciliation as a part of the operating procedure.
- Facilitates early detection of errors or prevention of frauds.

Example: Internal check system on payment of salary in an educational institution

√ One person prepares the pay bill of non-teaching staff

√ Another person checks calculations and makes entry in the books of accounts and prepares cheques.

√ Supervisor authorizes the payment.

√ Cashier makes the payment in cash/cheque.

Setting work standards and quantitative controls: It consists of specific policies and procedures that are put in place to minimize inefficient use of resources, non-compliance, etc.

Adequate documentation: Documents should be prepared and records should be maintained in such a manner that they are clearly comprehensible to all users. Documents need to be pre-numbered. Use of documents should be periodically verified for ensuring accountability.

Internal audit: The scope of internal auditing within an organization is broad and may involve activities that ascertain effectiveness of operations, the reliability of financial reporting, prevent, detect and investigate fraud, safeguard assets, and check compliance of the organisation with the established rules and regulations. In other words internal audit is an independent appraisal activity undertaken within an organization for the review of accounting, financial and other operations. It is carried out by staff specially assigned for it. Unlike external/ statutory audit, it is a continuous process. It leads to quality assurance. Internal auditors carry out post transaction review of operations and records. The general aim is to promote efficiency in the educational institution's financial control and management. Internal audit ascertains whether existing controls are adequate and effective, whether prescribed policies and procedures have been followed, whether resources of educational institution have been used efficiently and economically and whether assets of the educational institution are safeguarded properly.

What is the difference among internal check, internal audit and external audit? Internai audit and internal check are some of the measures adopted for ensuring internal control and these activities are carried out by employees of the organization unlike external audit carried out by outsiders. Through internal check the work of one employee automatically gets checked by another while the work is still on but in case of internal audit, after the work has been done by one, the other steps in to check it.

As managers of educational institutions you may adopt some measures for internal control as listed below:

- Creation of lines of authority and responsibility and manning the lines created with suitable staff.

- Framing financial policies and rules in keeping with the policies and legal provisions of the State.
- Making accounting system rigid as far as controls is concerned.
- Regularly and frequently calling for information on important aspects such as balance sheet, information pertaining to inflow of funds, variance from budgeted provisions, etc.
- Having dual control with safes and vaults to see that they open with keys in the possession of two people.
- Regularly checking inventories of physical assets.
- Engaging more people in carrying out and recording a transaction.
- Securing records in the computer with passwords and seeing to it that they cannot be tampered with.
- Changing people manning sensitive posts regularly.
- Cash being highly susceptible to misuse has to be safeguarded with measures like limited access to cash, surprise cash count, dual control over cash deposited, issuing receipts for even small amounts deposited, etc.
- Conveying to employees about zero tolerance towards fraud and misappropriations.
- Seeing that the generally accepted procedures of accounting are adhered to.
- Seeing that employees function as per their level of authorization.
- There is daily posting of records.
- Regular checking and balancing of relevant records.
- Numbering sequentially instruments used for items like cash receipt vouchers, checks, etc. to facilitate reconciling and control.
- Audit trail is created to trace a transaction from its beginning to its end.

Policy appraisals: Organizational policies also need periodical review so as to ensure that targets/standards set are achievable and can be implemented and the controls are achieving desired outcomes. Wherever, the gap is significant it needs to be analyzed for correction so that the goals of the educational institution are met.

We may summarize internal control through the following Figure 3.2:

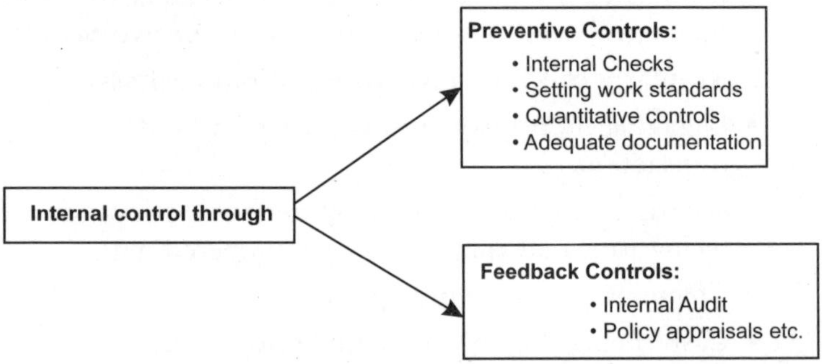

Figure 3.2: Internal Control

3.6 Audit Programme

For carrying out audit work effectively, an audit programme is first chalked out before actually commencing the audit work. An audit programme is a comprehensive outline or listing of the steps/specific audit procedures to be followed for the verification of books of accounts. It contains the audit objectives for each area along with detailed instructions for the audit staff. An audit programme essentially covers: (a) study of laws, regulations relating to constitution/formation of the educational institution, (b) familiarization with various aspects such as activities, organisation chart, list of records maintained, previous audit reports etc. of the educational institution, (c) review of past performance, (d) evaluation of internal controls, (e) verification of receipts, payments and assets and liabilities, (f) checking arithmetical accuracy of books of accounts, (g) preparation of audit report, etc.

Audit programmes depend upon the unique needs and circumstances of an institution. A specimen audit programme of an educational institution is as follows.

General considerations about the institution being audited:

- To obtain an overall picture of the financial position of the institution.
- Legislations/acts, regulations relating to the constitution /formation of the educational institution.
- Familiarization with various aspects such as activities, organisation chart, list of records maintained, previous audit reports, etc. of the institution.
- Studying the compliance of the institution with the prevailing policies, statutes, norms, rules and regulations governing it.
- Studying the Minutes of the meetings of the managing committee/executive council, finance committee, etc. on financial matters and the resolutions, their compliance and implications.
- Determining whether sufficient financial resources are available to support the delivery of each program offered including the student support services required for them.
- Determining whether the programmes offered are cost effective in terms of annual enrolment.
- Evaluating internal controls and their efficacy.
- Studying operation of bank accounts.
- Comparison of income and expenses projected in the budget and the variances there from.
- Checking arithmetical accuracy of books of accounts.

Verification of receipts

Verification of receipts from the various sources like grants, donations, fees, sale proceeds, interests, etc. and their accounting. Within this:

- Verification of students' fee register, counterfoils of receipts, class registers, cash/bank book and see that there is no inconsistency.

- Examination of the system of recovery of fines, late fees, etc.
- Ensuring that grants/donation/money raised for a particular purpose is spent accordingly.
- Verifying that caution money deposit is refunded.
- Confirming that caution money and other security deposits paid by students on admission have been shown as liability in the balance sheet and not transferred to revenue.
- Verifying that fines relating to late payment or absence, etc., have been collected and remitted under proper authority.
- Checking that hostel dues have been recovered before students' accounts are closed.
- In case amount of arrears on account of fees, hostel rents, etc. become substantial, reporting to the competent authority about it.
- Verifying whether the funds obtained/generated have been used for the designated purpose or lie unused and so on.
- To determine if refund of income tax have been claimed and recorded.

Verification of Payments

- To vouch the payment of salaries with reference to pay roll register, bank book and bank statement. Increments in salary if sanctioned have to be checked. For this reference may be made to copies of letters of appointment/agreement.
- To see that provident funds are deducted properly, rules and guidelines pertaining to them are followed and that the amount has been invested in appropriate securities.
- Studying the capital expenditures made, the nature of transaction and other details pertaining to them.
- Checking the fee concessions, scholarships and other benefits provided to learners.

- To check that income tax is deducted at source from the salary of the staff wherever it is necessary and the same deposited in the government exchequer.

Assets and liabilities: The following is required:

- Physical examination of assets like equipments for sports, technology, laboratory, library, etc. and the regular maintenance of stock registers and inventories, recording depreciation on depreciable assets, checking whether unserviceable assets have been written off. Liabilities of the institution if any also need to be studied.
- Verification of cash in hand and bank balance of the institution.
- Stock taking of assets and liabilities are necessary. Generally educational institutions enjoy exemptions from income tax, however refund of deduction of tax at source for dividends and other sources of income, if taxable and deposition into government exchequer of income tax deductions of employees whether being done properly is studied.
- Studying investments made by the institution

This is not an exhaustive list of items to be verified as every educational institution has a unique situation. Hence the items to be verified may differ.

An audit programme is prepared by external auditor but head of the educational institution should have awareness about this as this kind of planning is helpful even for internal audit.

3.7 Audit Report

In the earlier sections, we have observed that audit is an examination of books of accounts, relevant records and financial statements carried out in order to express an opinion thereon. We have discussed about the various techniques used by the auditor to gather evidence. Based on analysis of the information obtained and evidenced gathered, the auditor forms an opinion. Thus, the final stage in the audit process is the communication of the opinion formed to the client organization, which may be an educational institution, through a report. Audit report is thus the document through which an auditor communicates his/her opinion. We shall now discuss form and contents of audit report, types of audit opinion and study a specimen audit report.

Form and Content of an Audit Report

There cannot be any standard form of audit report that is applicable to all auditing situations. It depends upon the regulatory requirements or statutory provisions governing the organisation. Terms of reference relating to appointment of the auditor also specify the matters to be reported in the audit report. However, there are certain basic components that are present in any audit report. These are:

(i) **Title:** The document containing observation and opinion of the auditor is usually titled as 'Auditor's Report'.

(ii) **Disclosure of client's name:** The audit report discloses the name of the client, such as the educational institution in which audit has been carried out.

(iii) **Addressee:** The audit report needs to be addressed to the authority for which it is meant. Normally audit report is addressed to appointing authority such as the head of the educational institution or the governing body, say of the educational institution.

(iv) **Period of audit:** The audit report should specify the period covered i.e. financial year for which audit has been carried out. This will facilitate the user to identify the financial statements of the period covered.

(v) **Statement on matters required by Statute or regulatory requirements (if any):** Sometimes the Statute or Law governing the organization may require the auditor to comment/report on certain matters. Accordingly, the auditor has to deal with those aspects in the audit report.

(vi) **Opinion of Auditor:** This is the vital part of the audit report. In this part the auditor expresses his opinion, on the basis of evidence obtained during the course of audit, as to whether the Balance Sheet/statement of financial affairs and income and expenditure account, give a true and fair view of the financial position of the institution. Auditor also has to comment upon the strengths and/or weaknesses in the accounting system, deficiencies in the internal control system non-compliance with the regulatory requirements and accounting standards, etc.

(vii) **Signature:** The audit report should bear the signature of the auditor.

(viii) **Date and Place of Signature:** The date of signing the report and name of the location, where report is signed should be mentioned in the audit report.

Types of auditor's opinion

Auditor's opinion may be unqualified, adverse or qualified. At times the auditor may not express any opinion. Where the auditor expresses his/her opinion without any reservation/ objection it is called unqualified opinion. On the contrary, in case of adverse opinion the auditor does not agree with state of affairs and working results. Therefore, he/she categorically says that Balance Sheet/Statement of affairs and Income and Expenditure Account do not reflect a true and fair view of the financial position. Third category is qualified opinion. Under this situation the auditor agrees with the audit propositions to a major extent subject to certain reservations. Thus, the auditor may say that subject to their observations, financial statements of the educational institution reflect a true and fair view of the state of affairs.

Specimen Audit Report

Auditors' Report on the Accounts of

XYZ College for the year ended 31st March, 2011

To

The Managing Committee of XYZ College

We have audited the attached Balance Sheet of XYZ College as at 31st March 2011 and also the Income and Expenditure Account and Receipts and Payments Accounts for the year ended on that date annexed thereto. These financial statements are the responsibility of the college management. Our responsibility is to express an opinion on these financial statements based on our audit. We conducted our audit in accordance with auditing standards generally accepted in India.

Those Standards require that we plan and perform the audit to obtain reasonable assurance about whether the financial statements are free of material misstatement. An audit includes examining, on a test basis, evidence supporting the amounts and disclosures in the financial statements. An audit also includes assessing the accounting principles used and significant estimates made by management, as well as evaluating the overall financial statement presentation. We believe that our audit provides a reasonable basis for our opinion.

Further, we report that we have obtained all the information and explanations, which to the best of our knowledge and belief were necessary for the purposes of our audit and in our opinion, proper books of accounts have been kept by the Management so far as appears from our examination of those books and the Balance Sheet, Income and Expenditure Account dealt with by this report are in agreement with the books of account subject to our separate notes on accounts.

In our opinion and to the best of our information and as per the explanations furnished to us, the said accounts give a true and fair view, subject to our separate Notes on Accounts attached herewith:

(a) In the case of the Balance Sheet, of the state of affairs of the College as at 31st March, 2011 and

(b) In the case of the Income and Expenditure Account, of the excess of Income over Expenditure for the year ended on that date.

Date: June16, 2011

For ABC & Associates
Place: New Delhi
Chartered Accountants
(Membership No. ....)

Notes on Accounts:
Specimen

XYZ College

Notes on Accounts— Forming part of Audit Report for the period ended on 31st March 2011

1. Fixed Assets

(a) Fixed Assets Registers: Fixed Assets Register is not being maintained with full details and description of assets. The authority should implement the system of physical verification of assets at least once in a year.

(b) Charging of depreciation: No depreciation is charged on assets as per prevailing practice of the college. Accordingly, the surplus during the period under review does not represent the true position without charging depreciation and is against the normal practice of accounting; thereby value of assets does not also show the actual position as on that date. The authority should implement the system of charging the depreciation on assets and excess/deficit of Income & Expenditure account should be drawn up accordingly.

2. Subsidy Fund

It has been observed that different sub-funds have been created but no separate bank accounts are maintained.

3. Current Liabilities

(a) Municipal Tax: It has been observed that municipal tax of ₹ 75,000 is lying outstanding for a long time. The Management of the College should take appropriate action for settlement of the said dues, otherwise adjust/write off the same account.

(b) House Rent for Student's Hostel: It has been observed that ₹ 15,000 has been shown as liability for a long time. Necessary action may be taken for proper write off of the same account.

4. The following information as required during the period under audit is attached as per separate annexes:

(i) Fees Structure
(ii) Student Strength
(iii) Faculty & Non-teaching staff Strength
(iv) Stock of Library Books
(v) Name-wise statement of provident fund balance

Date: June16, 2011

For ABC & Associates
Place: New Delhi
Chartered Accountants
(Membership No. ....)

Suppose queries are raised in the audit report. What is to be done? In such cases the following steps may be taken:

- Submit further information (evidences) on issues on which queries have been raised and respond satisfactorily to the queries raised.
- Consider measures such as reviewing assets against liabilities, writing off bad debts etc.
- In the trial balance check the figures, calculations, debtors and creditors, entry of all the accounts books to the trial balance.
- Going over the cashbook and other financial documents and financial statements to locate the errors pointed out and take corrective actions.

3.8 Summary

Auditing is a process of collection and evaluation of evidence for the purpose of reporting on economic information. The economic information may include financial statements such as balance sheet, profit and loss account, income and expenditure, etc. costing statements like cost sheet, variance analysis statement, etc. and statements prepared to facilitate managerial control such as statements showing actual performance vis a vis targets. Auditing is thus a systematic periodic, independent and methodical examination and evaluation of financial systems, and financial information like accounts, tax returns, and other financial records. The main objective of auditing of financial statements is to ascertain as to whether the financial statements, of an organization, which may also be an educational institution, reflect a true and fair view of the financial position and working results at the end of an accounting period. It aims to collect and evaluate audit evidence to form and communicate to the users of the financial statements, an audit opinion, expressed as a formal report. Detection of errors and fraud is not the primary objective of auditing but is incidental to the main objective of auditing. Errors may be unintentional and can be of different types such as omission, commission, errors of duplication, compensation and fraud, which may be committed by various means, etc. Auditing also intends to detect, correct as well as prevent fraud. Audit is thus an instrument of financial control. It determines the fairness with which an organisation has presented its financial statements and acts as a safeguard for the stakeholders against extravagance, carelessness or fraud in financial matters.

There are different stages in an audit engagement. Each stage involves critical decisions on the part of the auditor. The stages are audit planning, evaluation of internal control, substantive testing, forming an opinion and reporting. Auditing aims to gather evidences about the financial information provided by the organization. The evidence collected should ideally be adequate, useful, relevant and persuasive. The evidence also has to be logically related to the audit objectives. Various techniques may be involved in auditing such as determining the accuracy of arithmetical calculations, vouching, examination of documents, inquiry, physical verification, etc.

Auditing is carried out by external agencies but it is also done by employees, i.e. internal auditing. Internal check and other measures like internal audit are adopted by the organization to acquire internal control. Internal audit and internal check are some of the measures adopted for ensuring internal control and these activities are carried out by employees of the organization unlike external audit carried out by outsiders. Through Internal check the work of one employee automatically gets checked by another while the work is still on but in case of internal audit, after the work has been done by one, the other steps in to check it.

For carrying out audit work effectively, an audit programme is first chalked out before actually commencing the audit work. An audit programme is a comprehensive outline with listing of the steps and specific audit procedures to be followed for the auditing. It may also outline the scope of the work to be performed by the audit team, the extent to which checks need to be carried out and the like. The final stage in the audit process is the communication of the opinion formed to the client organization, which may be an educational institution through a report. Audit report is thus the document through which an auditor communicates his opinion.

3.9 Self Assessment

3.9.1 *Questions*

Answer the following questions.

1. Do you think going for audit is beneficial for an institution? Why?
2. What are the desirable qualities of auditors?
3. Discuss the common types of errors that an auditor may detect in accounting.
4. Will you have internal auditing in your institution? Why?
5. Is it beneficial to have internal check system? Discuss its role.

3.9.2 *Clues*

1. Audit helps in efficient financial management. It helps to detect and prevent errors and frauds, enhances accuracy, authenticity and reliability of the books of accounts and financial statements, keeps the staff careful, vigilant and keep information up to date, makes financial information acceptable for legal purposes (for details see Section 3.3.1).
2. Possessing necessary qualifications and personal qualities (for details sec Section 3.3.3).
3. Errors of omission, errors of commission, compensating errors, etc. (for details see Section 3.3.1).
4. For checking accounting, financial and other operations (for details see Section 3.5).
5. A system of internal check is an arrangement of staff duties whereby no one person is allowed to carry through

and record every aspect of a transaction so that, without collusion between two or more persons, fraud is prevented and at the same time, the possibilities of errors are reduced to a minimum (for details see Section 3.5).

3.10 Activities

You may carry out these activities for gaining a better understanding of this chapter.

1. Study the system of internal control through internal auditing and internal check adopted by any two educational institutions and prepare a report on it.
2. Collect audit reports of any three educational institutions and study them.

References

Commonwealth Secretariat (1993). *Better Schools, Resource Materials for School Heads in Africa*. Module 5—Financial Management. Commonwealth Secretariat, UNESCO: London

Gupta, K. and Arora, A. (1996). *Fundamentals of Auditing*. New Delhi: Tata McGraw Hill Publishing Company Ltd.

ICWAI, (2002). Study Notes—*Auditing*. Directorate of Studies, Kolkata.

Tandon, B.N. (1978). *Practical Auditing*. New Delhi: S.Chand and Company Ltd..

Website (Websites may not be permanent)

http://www.isect.com/html/ca_faq.html.

http://www.auditservices.com/aevidence.html

http://www.oamcc.com/pdfs/13%20-%20Auditing.pdf

Budgeting

4

4.1 Introduction

In the earlier chapters, we have discussed aspects related to accounting and auditing. In this chapter we shall have a discourse on a very important aspect of financial management—budgeting. In a layman's language it could be said that those managing an organization have to prepare a budget so as to ensure that the income of the organization and the expenses incurred are in sync with each other. This will ensure that the funds available do not lie unused, nor do the expenses tend to overshoot the income. However, as you study this chapter, you will find that this is an oversimplified assertion and there is much more to it. As a budget provides the framework within which all financial transactions of the organization are to be carried out, it is essential for the administrators of all organizations including educational institutions to possess the basic know how about budgeting and administering it. In this chapter, we shall discuss first the definition of budget and its importance, types of budget, approaches to budgeting, process of budgeting, budgetary control and a few other aspects about budgeting.

4.2 Objectives

Following a study of this chapter, you are expected to:

- explain the concept of budget;
- state the importance of budgeting;
- discuss the types of budgets;
- describe the approaches to budgeting; and
- explain budgetary control.

4.3 What is a Budget?

The term budget is widely used and even in our daily life we use it. For instance, we at times say 'my budget will not permit it'. Or a principal of a college may tell her students 'setting up a gym is beyond our budget'. We also know that the Finance Minister and the Railways Minister present the annual budgets every year. Thus budgets are prepared regularly at the national level, in various organizations, and even at the household level, of course with varying degrees of complexity and sophistication. But what is exactly meant by a budget? Let us first try to understand the term 'budget'. The dictionary definition of a budget as an estimate or plan of expenditure in relation to income gives an idea about a budget but it is too simplistic. A budget is a fiscal plan formulated to reach the goals of an organization. The fiscal plan includes the organization's expected incomes and proposed expenditures over a certain period of time. It is thus a comprehensive and coordinated documented plan of the estimated expenditures and revenue of an organization expressed in financial terms. Since the operations and the proposed estimates are either yet to be undertaken or are those that have already been undertaken but require to be continued in future, therefore budgets like any other plan are for future, made for a specific period. A budget is thus a mechanism for effective management of an organization. It is a plan that helps in developing strategies to attain the objectives and goals of the organization.

Now that you have an idea about a budget, let us now define a budget. A budget is a fiscal expression, rather a comprehensive and coordinated plan, expressed in financial terms, which outlines the organisation's operations to be undertaken vis-a-vis the resources available for a specific period in the future. It thus outlines an organization's operational goals vis-a-vis its financial position. It is thus a financial document used to project future income and expenses but for operational purposes it is an action plan of the organisation aimed at, evaluating performance, allocating resources and formulating plans.

What should be the significant features of the budget that you prepare? The budget of your institution should turn out to be not just a financial document but go beyond it to offer a realistic estimate regarding the income and thus reduces uncertainties by reigning in expenses in excess of income of your organization while simultaneously checking underutilization of resources. It should provide the summary of the intended expenditures with the proposals of the incomes to meet them. It should thus serve as a tool for exercising control over financial transactions of the organization and reflect the aspirations of the organization and the means available to realize them. As rightly mentioned by Chandra (2003) a budget is the principal device to compel and discipline management planning. Enaohwo (1990) had underlined that a budget is the main framework for financial management and it provides the essential pathways through which the financial resources of the school could be harnessed for attaining the objectives that have been set. The same thing could be said about all educational institutions including those at the tertiary level.

When is the budget to be prepared? For what period of time should the budget be prepared? A budget is usually prepared for a specified time period, the budget period. However, midterm revisions are at times made to accommodate pressing needs. Budget period, is usually of one year—1st April to 31st March i.e. a financial year. Most organizations divide their budget period into calendar months (or periods). However the yearly budget may be divided into quarterly or even monthly budgets (Chandra, 2003).

What are the important things to be remembered while you prepare budget? During budget preparation, prioritization of activities is needed as per the returns expected from them. However you need to remember that such prioritization should be within the framework of the financial resources, government policies, social and educational relevance. Budgeting basically involves setting up fiscal targets, formulating expenditure policies, allocating resources as per the policies and fiscal target, monitoring the budget prepared, etc. If you study the budget of an organization, you will find that there is an attempt to balance the expenses with the income. There may rather be attempts to keep expenses lower than the income to develop a corpus of surplus funds and this would be a prudent approach for an educational institution. The act of balancing requires exerting control over the operations to be undertaken and this in turn calls for practices like prioritizing needs, mobilizing resources, controlling costs by adopting cost effective techniques, etc. As per the Commonwealth Secretariat (1993) it is advisable to have a budget that promotes cost effectiveness with high level of institutional output, at low levels of expenditure. This holds good for all educational institutions.

4.3.1 *Importance of budgeting*

Now that you have a concept of budget and its need let us concretize the major reasons that justify the exercise for budgeting. In other words, the major benefits that you would attain through budgeting are as follows:

- The budget is a tool for management by objectives (to increase organizational performance by identification of common goals and the objectives comprising them throughout the organization).
- It is a formal way of communicating plans and objectives and suggesting the means available to attain them, to the various units of the organization so that they are understood and pursued. Thus the budget is potent to direct and coordinate various efforts and operations of the organization towards the attainment of the common goals.
- It reflects not only the goals but also the time schedule for the fulfillment of various objectives and also the responsibility and accountability of the units and individuals and thus acts as a device for control.
- Output of the various units of the organization can be assessed and necessary corrective measures can be adopted if deviations from budgeted amounts are detected.
- It enlists all the sources of funds that can be available and ensures that the use of resources is maximized.

- A budget monitors financial transactions of the organization and reigns in expenses in excess of income. It also helps in keeping track of income, expenses, savings and borrowings of the organisation.
- Provides a detailed plan of action thus reducing uncertainty and directs individual and group efforts to achieve the goals of an organization.
- It helps in coordination i.e. striking a balance between workers, teachers, academic and non academic staff in case of educational institutions, material and other resources and also in maintaining a harmony in the working of various departments of the organization and thus saves efforts and resources (Pandey, 1983).

  An Illustration: If printed material is to be produced in bulk, the department responsible for printing of study material should not give the go ahead to production unless the purchase cell has procured the necessary materials like paper, art card, etc. Similarly purchase cell should not procure paper that will not be used for production.
- Serves as a standard against which the actual performance may be judged (Chandra, 2003). It is thus a tool for evaluation of the financial performance of the organization.

Thus budget requires informed decision making. It helps to review the current fiscal position, identify the aims of the institution, prioritize needs, monitor progress and establish mechanism for collective management for attaining aims of the institution. Usually in an educational institution budgets are prepared for different departments or units on the basis of the budgeting guidelines developed by the budget committee of the institution. For instance, departments of science, social science, languages, performing arts, administration, admission, examinations, student support, etc. may prepare their own budgets. Even within the departments, faculty may provide budgets for their own programmes. It is important that there is coordination among the various units of the institution and also of the units within the departments/centers of the institution. In the absence of coordination there would be just a compilation of projected expenses during a fiscal period, rather than a budget. The danger with this approach is that the essential functions of a budget viz. planning expenses in the light of the resources available, cost effectiveness, prioritization and the like are ignored.

It is better to have a budget (or a finance) committee in an institution that makes a schedule for budget preparation by various units and the master budget, provides necessary information for budgeting, sees to the coordination of the unit budgets, reconciles inconsistencies in them, develops the master budget for the entire institution and sends it for approval to the management. It may also compare the results with the budgetary provisions and investigates the variances.

4.3.2 *Essentials of budgeting*

Successful and sound budgeting is based upon certain prerequisites. Let us study these essentials now.

- **Budgets are prepared to achieve the objective of the organization:** Those involved in budgeting must possess complete knowledge of the nature, targets and the resources of the organization. Adequate and correct information on these aspects are essential for budgeting (Jhamb, 2008). Budgeting is based on the objectives and goals of the institution which are drawn from the dynamic socio-economic and technological aspirations. Therefore goals and objectives change and so does the premises for budgeting.
- **Within the framework of the policies and goals:** An educational institution has to adopt a financial plan that does not contradict the policies of the state and the established financial rules and regulations. Also, a budget has to be within the broad framework of the goals of the organization and the strategic planning done by the organization to achieve the goals.
- **Unambiguous basis:** A budget is based on clear cut objectives and well established goals of the institution rather than ambiguous projections that are hard to

translate into fiscal terms. For instance, aiming at improving instructional practices, though desirable but being an abstraction it will hardly make any sense for budgeting. Rather we need to specify the measures that improve instructional practices like investment in technology, recruitment of teachers, investing in laboratories, and the like. The expenses on these can be spelt out in concrete terms.

- **Realistic estimates:** The budget as a fiscal plan should include estimates and propositions regarding receipts and expenses that are realistic in nature. The figures should be estimated with objectivity. All anticipated costs must be allocable, consistent and documented (see the concepts and conventions of accounting in the chapter on accounting).
- **Accounting System:** Budgeting depends heavily upon the data generated by the accounting system of the institution. However the data may have to be processed to facilitate the budgetary functions of planning and control for the budget period. For example if a particular amount is depicted as per capita grant during a particular year, while making a budgetary estimate on this account, it would be necessary to project the probable student strength during the budget period and the ensuing revenue on this account.
- **Decentralized process:** In educational institutions, for a budget to be more realistic, those working at the ground level, i.e. the teachers need to be involved in the budgeting process. A committee that prepares the budget should have teachers in it. A fiscal plan thus developed would have wider acceptance and hence would be easier to implement. Therefore, teachers and other employees involved in budgeting should be provided with the know-how of budgeting.
- **Flexibility:** The budgeting system should be flexible enough to take the benefit of the opportunities that may arise during the budget period but are not covered by

the budget. Otherwise not only would the fund generated later remain unused while a pressing need remains unfulfilled but also impair the initiative and freedom of the administrative head and the teachers. It is also to be seen that a budget should not become merely an accounting document dictated by book keeping activities (Nelson & Purdey 1971; 1977 as cited in Orlosky, McCleary, Shapiro & Webb 1984). However, such flexibility should be introduced with prudence.

4.4 Types of Budgets

The comprehensive master budget covers all facets of the operations and finances. It usually has the operating and the financial budgets. Within these types there may be many types of budgets.

Operating budget: These types of budget pertain to the impact of operating decisions mainly like production, sales and purchases. It includes different types of budgets like the sales budget, production budget, purchase budget, etc. Although purchase of materials, production, sales and profit making were not common in educational institutions, today entrepreneurship in educational institutions is welcomed (see Chapter 1). There are many educational institutions, especially those operating in the distance mode that produce educational resources and market them. Educational institutions may purchase materials like paper, produce outputs like prospectus, forms, content in electronic and print media, etc. in huge quantities, sell them, even with some profit. Many agricultural universities are also marketing their products.

A budget for operating expenses depends on the sales budget. Sales budget is the building block of an operational budget. It depicts sales volume and selling prices for each type of product. It is prepared on certain premises such as demand for a certain type of output, past and emerging trends, sales promotion efforts of the institution, etc.

Example of Revenue Budget (e.g. Sale of study materials) for the first quarter of the financial year....

Product	April ₹	May ₹	June ₹	Total ₹
Prospectus	900	1,050	1,200	3,150
Printed courseware	15,750	16,800	17,850	50,400
Total	16,650	17,850	19,050	53,550

A sales budget requires survey of customer needs, (in educational institutions, especially those for higher education, the needs of target groups, i.e. student's needs for courses may be ascertained. It may be determined whether investment in developing and delivering a course would be worthwhile. If there is demand for the course among prospective students, the course may be launched) and statistical analysis to predict demands. However, educational organisations not being business organisations and not being supposed to sell product/services are usually not involved in these activities.

The sales budget provides an outline of the volume of sales. We then need to set a budget for the expenses that will be incurred in producing that volume. This budget categorizes expenses into two main areas—the first is the operational costs which include such things as the components and supplies used to produce the product, or services provided. The second is the administration costs that are non-operational costs and will include things such as marketing, human resources, logistics, as well as cost for general administration. Unlike in industries, in educational institutions the operational costs for production is not so relevant but for distance education institution with industrialised functioning there could be some areas in which such costs are relevant. For example, for printing self learning materials in bulk, the amount of paper to be procured and costs involved need to be considered. Non operational costs would involve for example, the printing charges, expenses for packaging and delivery of materials, etc.

A production budget may be made by adding the budgeted sales depicted in the sales budget to the targeted ending finished goods inventory and deducting from this the beginning finished goods inventory. In other words, Budgeted production units = (sales estimates) + (expected ending inventory)—(Beginning inventory). It is thus a plan for the saleable materials to be produced in accordance with the sales forecast for each type of product.

Example of production budget in units for the first quarter of the financial year.... (Adapted from Pandey, 1983)

No. of (Units)	January	February	March
Estimated sale of prospectus	900	1,050	1,200
+ desired ending inventory	840	960	1,080
	1,740	2,010	2,280
–beginning inventory	720	840	960
Units of brochure to be produced	1020	1,170	1,320
Estimated sales of printed courseware A	2,250	2,400	2,550
+ desired ending inventory	1,920	2,040	2,160
	4,170	4,440	4,710
– beginning inventory	1,800	1,920	2,040
Units of printed courseware to be produced	2,370	2,520	2,670

Thereafter the purchase budget is prepared. It depicts the material required for production manufacturing and the purchase scheme. The material usage depends upon the level of production and the beginning inventory and the desired ending inventories. The units of materials to be purchased can be determined by the formula:

Purchase (units) = Budgeted usage + desired ending inventory – beginning inventory

Example of a material purchase budget for the first quarter of the financial year .....

(Adapted from Pandey, 1983).

No. of (Units)	January	February	March
Material for producing prospectus	2,040	2,340	2,640
Material for producing printed courseware B	9,480	10,080	10,680
Total production needs	11,520	12,420	13,320
+ desired ending balance	17,280	18,630	19,980
Total needs	28,800	31,050	33,300
–beginning balance	15,750	17,280	18,630
Purchase	13,050	13,770	14,670
Cost of purchases	₹ 13,050	₹ 13,770	₹ 14,670

Financial Budget: The financial budget depicts the financial implications of the operating budget, i.e. the expected inflow and outflow of cash. It includes the capital expenditure budget, the cash budget and the budgeted balance sheet (Chandra, 2004).

Capital expenditure budget: Capital expenditures is the financial investment required by capital items or fixed assets to be procured by an organization like campus, buildings, equipment, etc. Capital expenditures to be budgeted include replacement, acquisition, or construction of plants, costly equipments, etc. Capital Expenditure Budget is a plan prepared for individual capital expenditure projects. It includes the capital projects in which investments would be made by the organization during the budget period along with their estimated costs and justifications. Suppose an educational institution wants a new physical asset like a building, a campus, a laboratory, computerization of a unit, etc. that requires planned investment, then a budget depicting the same may be prepared.

Example of Capital expenditure budget

(₹)	April	May	June
Purchase Equipments	10000	–	–
Purchase furniture	–	5000	5000

Cash Budget: It depicts the inflow and outflow of cash during the budget period. The inflow could be from fee, sale of prospectus, forms, educational and other saleable outputs, sale of equipments or other assets, rent collected from assets rented out, interest accrued, borrowings, donations, etc.

An example of a cash flow budget is detailed below.

Cash flow budget of ABC Institution for the financial year 2009-2010

	April	May	June
Income (₹)			
Sales	4000	2500	4000
Other Income	2000	0500	1000
Total	**6000**	**3000**	**5000**
Payments (₹)			
Creditors	2000	3000	2000
Other Payments	1000	1000	500
Purchase/Hire of Fixed Assets	3000	500	500
Total	**6000**	**4500**	**3000**
Bank Account (₹)			
Opening Balance at Month Start	2000	2000	500
+ Total Income	6000	3000	5000
– Total Payments	6000	4500	3000
Balance at Month End	**2000**	**500**	**2500**

The annual budget may be broken down into monthly, and even weekly, estimates of cash flow. The importance of managing cash is paramount as poor cash flow management can have serious effects.

Budgeted Balance Sheet: It shows the financial position of the organisation at the year end. Projected assets, liabilities and the owner's equity at the end of the budget period are depicted. The difference between the assets and liabilities in the budget forms the owner's equity. It indicates the worth of the business held by the owners after taking into account the debts (if any).

Example of Budgeted Balance Sheet

Assets	₹
Cash	9,00,000
Debtors	30,000
Inventory	3,00,000
Buildings	10,00,000
Plant and Equipment	4,00,000
Investments	7,00,000
Total Assets	**33,30,000**
– Liabilities	
Creditors	2,00,000
Loans	1,20,000
Total Liabilities	3,20,000
Owner's Equity	**30,10,000**

You may be wondering whether these budgets are applicable to educational institutions. Today many education institutions, especially those offering distance education have an industrialised operational system with need survey (similar to market research) to determine the demand for a programme followed by planning and development of educational programmes. There is also bulk production of print and audio-video materials and their delivery. Therefore, all these types of budgets may need to be prepared.

4.5 Approaches to Budgeting

There can be various approaches to budgeting. The traditional approach to budgeting, i.e, incremental budgeting was popular earlier. But later modern approaches emerged. We shall discuss both these approaches so that the differences are clear.

Incremental budgeting: It is also known as traditional or line item budgeting. The previous financial year's budget is considered for this approach to budgeting and held as the base line from which the next budget is to be prepared. It is assumed that the amounts depicted in the previous year's budget would have to be increased to some extent to get the current budget. The assumptions for such increases are inflation, need for hike in pay of the employees, etc. This kind of budgeting was quite popular earlier till alternative approaches emerged. It is also known as traditional budgeting. It allocates expenses into categories of inputs and summarizes expenses in gross terms. It is thus input oriented and budgeted financial statement elements are grouped by administrative entities and objects like salary, maintenance, providing instructions, library, laboratories, etc. Therefore, it is also called 'object budget' since expenditure is broken down in an object wise manner.

This approach to budgeting is simple. It is easily prepared and requires relatively simple calculations. It is also easy to explain it to the stakeholders as there is a simple rationale for it, which is the assumption that the amounts depicted in the previous year's budget would have to be increased to some extent to get the current budget. However, this approach has certain weaknesses. It simply considers the inflow of funds from various sources, like grants, fees, sales, etc. and expenditures like salaries, rent, telephone bills, etc. and tries to balance these two. But there is hardly any scope for interpreting the cost of providing a particular service or obtaining a particular outcome. In other words, we may say that this approach does not relate costs to the impact.

Since estimates for enlisted items are included in this approach, hence it is commonly called 'line-item classification'. 'What' is purchased rather than 'why' it is done takes prominence in this kind of budgeting. The financial outlay is merely depicted without trying to interrelate it to the programmes and the achievements visualized. It does not therefore help the administration to appraise the outcome of the different schemes, programmes or activities in which investment has been made. Hence it does not serve as an adequate basis for informed decision-making (Bhatnagar & Agrawal, 1997). A line-item budget is basically a tool for controlling expenditures as it spells out the level of spending allowed for specific purposes.

This approach to budgeting projects the activities of the past budget into future ones thereby justifying them. This approach leaves hardly any scope for change and new initiatives. Secondly there is isolation of the activities pertaining to estimating from that of policy making. In other words, financial planning is not linked to strategic planning. Thus this type of budgeting does not reflect the cost benefit analysis and value for money. This approach to budgeting which lacks strong linkages between propositions and their objectives is mechanical in nature.

Line item approach to budgeting thus suffers certain limitations, such as:

- The previous financial year's budget is considered to be ideal and a model basing on which the next budget is to be built.
- Higher or lower funding than that actually required for a particular activity will continue in the next year without any scope for rectifying it.
- May encourage units to demand increased budget every year and individuals to demand a pay hike every year.
- It will not encourage units to exercise economy as next year's budget would definitely bring more money.
- It cannot accommodate new activities like new courses or new level of an existing activity as for example sudden increase in enrolment. Therefore, new initiatives may take a back seat with this approach to budgeting.

Example

Description	2009-10	2010-11
	Budget amount (₹)	Budget Amount (₹)
Salary of teachers	6,00,000	6,20,000
Salary of Supporting Staff	40,000	50,000
Maintenance of infrastructure	28,000	30,000
Laboratory	1,00,000	1,30,000
Print medium	80,000	1,00,000
Electronic medium	20,000	25,000
Total	**8,68,000**	**9,55,000**

Program Budgeting

Program budget is a fiscal plan related to the programs or the major activities undertaken by an institution like teaching, student support, evaluation, etc. It establishes the programmes, their objectives, costs, i.e. resources and the expected results. The allocation of resources is not merely an input but is a part of the systems approach applied to the intuitional functioning. There is a thus PPBS (Planning, Programming, Budgeting System) in operation. With a clear picture of the cost of the programmes in relation to the outcomes of the programme, this approach to budgeting gives vital clues as to the need to continue, modify, suspend or terminate a programme. It also guides prioritization of programmes and imparts transparency. It includes the following aspects (Orlosky, McCleary, Shapiro & Webb 1984):

- Grouping of all efforts and activities into programs such as transportation, food, physical education, etc.
- Establishing the major goals of each programme.
- Mentioning specifically the objectives that on achievement would ensure the accomplishment of the larger goals.
- Establishing alternatives for achieving goals of the programmes.
- Comparing costs and effectiveness for alternatives of attaining the goals of the programmes.
- Establishing evaluation criteria to measure the success of each programme.
- Allocating resources for each programme to accomplish its goals.

Example of Program Budget (Adapted from Orlosky, *et al.*1984).

Programme	Teacher	Supporting Staff	Text Books	Library	Audio Visual Aids	Supplies	Total Cost by Program
Instruction	**(₹)**	**(₹)**	**(₹)**	**(₹)**	**(₹)**	**(₹)**	**(₹)**
Languages	3,00,000	50,000	30,000	50,000	20,000	2000	4,52,000
Science	3,00,000	50,000	40,000	50,000	60,000	3000	5,03,000
Mathematics	3,00,000	50,000	30,000	50,000	20,000	4000	4,54,000
Social Studies	1,00,000	50,000	40,000	60,000	10,000	3000	2,63,000

Performance Based Budgeting

Performance budgeting is similar to program budgeting but it emphasizes outcomes. Statements of missions, goals and objectives included in this approach justify the investments as resources are allocated to achieve specific objectives based on program goals. Performance budgets use statements of missions, goals and objectives to explain why the money is being spent (Young, 2003). This new budgeting method goes beyond the traditional methods of analyzing and utilizing budget figures. In traditional budgeting approach long-term plans are broken into annual budgets. At the end of the budget period budget figures are matched with actual results and the variance is calculated for revising monetary amounts for the next budgeting cycle. It has a rudimentary role in monitoring performance. But in performance based budgeting we decide on objectives and spell out activities that are carried out to achieve the objectives.

Key Performance Indicators (KPIs) are identified at the outset for this kind of budgeting and are linked to resources. This is similar to the Corporate Performance Management framework of management used for tracking progress of a work. This kind of linking resource with results provides information on costs involved in getting a particular outcome. For instance, the expense involved in purchasing printers vis-a-vis the money saved in getting materials printed from external sources may be considered.

This approach to budgeting involves the process of analyzing, identifying, simplifying and crystallizing specific performance objectives of an activity to be completed over a period, in the framework of the organizational objectives, the purpose and objectives of the job. Thus performance budgeting is a system of budgeting which states operations in terms of functions and activities. It involves evaluation of programmes and performance appraisal is central to this kind of budgeting. It attempts to match monetary cost and benefit of the programme and gives the definite scope of the activity and its cost. It helps in providing a sound and systematic system of reporting with evaluation of each programme and thus facilitates decision making. It is management by objective and brings accountability for the actions taken (Jhamb, 2008). However, the limitations of this kind of budgeting could be that carrying out qualitative appraisal of programmes is difficult. Moreover evaluation of activities and products in educational institutions is difficult as tangible activities and products may be elusive. For instance learning with the help of technology is an abstraction. Even if it does not lead to better learning outcomes, would finding fault with technology, stopping investment in it and reverting to chalk and talk method of teaching be the right approach?

What are the benefits of this approach to budgeting? This approach to budgeting is a way to allocate resources to achieve specific objectives based on program goals and measured results. Three things are important in this type of budgeting—namely the result, the strategy to attain the results and the activities for achieving the results. It links the funds budgeted with the results expected and thus improves the internal management of the resources. This approach to budgeting links a financial plan with the strategic plan of the organisation. It helps in policy making because of its result oriented approach. The objectives and activities specified make evaluation of the cost effectiveness of the activities possible and thus help in strategic planning. However, considerable time and effort are required for preparing it.

An illustration of Performance Budget

WQ University had got the profit plan for the year 2010-11 approved by the Budget Committee from sale of printed self learning materials produced by it. It involved selling 2,40,000 units annually at a selling Price of ₹ 100 per unit. The budgeted variable cost of production was ₹ 40 per unit and the quarterly fixed costs were budgeted at ₹ 20,00,000. Thus the planned annual income was ₹ 64,00,000. Due to non-availability of the requisite amount of paper only 50,000 units could be produced and sold in the second quarter. There was an increase in the variable cost of production by ₹ 5 per unit. In order to improve the production process, an expenditure of ₹ 2,00,000 was incurred. The selling price was increased by ₹ 10 per unit.

Solution

Performance Budget of WQ University

(For the Second quarter period July 01, 2011 to September 30, 2011)

Details	Original Budget (₹)	Budget for Actual Activity (₹)	Revised Budget (₹)
Sale (Unit)	**60000**	**50000**	**50000**
Sales Value	6000000	5000000	5500000
Less: Variable Cost	2400000	2000000	2450000
Contribution	3600000	3000000	3050000

Zero Based Budgeting

Zero Based Budgeting (ZBB) is a relatively new concept in budgeting method. As against traditional incremental budgeting with a 'budget creep', ZBB starts with zero as the base line. Each programme or activity has to be justified and each year a budget from a zero base has to be constructed by providing new objectives, evaluation criteria and justifications (Orlosky, McCleary, Shapiro & Webb, 1984). ZBB considers the effectiveness of an activity afresh and the previous year's resource allocation is not automatically the basis of the current year's allocation. Instead, there is a need to justify anew the entire budget request. If it is found to be ineffective or inefficient, it can be eliminated or scaled down or modified. Continuation of an activity also has to be justified. It also allows new activities unlike incremental budget. Prioritization of activities is done in terms of their ability to fulfill the goals of the organization and cost involved and then only funds are allocated. Thus there is objectivity in budgeting. Unlike incremental budgeting, future rather than past is important and this type of budget can therefore, accommodate changes. Moreover, only the economically viable projects are prioritized. However preparing it is relatively difficult as carrying out cost benefit analysis of each of the activities is a time consuming affair.

ZBB is a tool for Management by Objectives. Cost benefit analysis carried out seeks effective but economic alternative and justification of the money spent and thus helps in reducing wasteful expenditure. In the conventional budgeting system budgets are based on trends or historical level of expenditure, i.e. it is based on the concept of incremental basis and the figures of the previous budget, forms the basis of the budget being prepared. However, the activities per se are not assessed for their efficiency. But under ZBB all activities are evaluated every time budget is prepared. For a ZBB, therefore, we break down each activity of the institution into 'decision packages', carry out the evaluation of the various activities and rank them in order of the benefits they will bring to the educational institution and then allocate resources as per the benefits accrued.

The budgeting process starts at zero as base requiring all expenditures to be completely justified instead of the traditional approach that allows a certain amount of money as expenditure at the base. Budget requests for the appropriations of funds are accepted on the basis of cost-benefit analysis which ensures value for money. Those activities which are of no value find no place in the budget even though these might have been an integral part of previous budget. ZBB thus attempts to weed out those activities which are not essential for the organization. For instance, if an organization does not use type writers or chalk boards any longer, ZBB will discontinue expenditure on them. Hence, the focus shifts from 'how' to expend to why to 'expend'. Budgeting though becomes time consuming and difficult. It becomes more efficient as there is effective utilization of resources and reduction of wasteful expenditures. The activities on which the organization was losing money as well as inflated requests for funds are eliminated. It introduces accountability and regulates expenditures as per prioritized needs.

The steps you may adopt for preparing ZBB are the following:

- Defining the objectives;
- Ignoring pre-existing budgets and preparing a fresh budget taking the base as nil/zero;
- Critically examine each item of expenditure in the fresh budget on the basis of their merit and hence desirability;
- Considering and evaluating alternative courses of action to compare the prices i.e. performing a cost-benefit analysis before deciding to allocate money on an item;
- Selecting the alternative found to be cost effective and needed by the organization.

While incremental line item budgeting does have some inherent weaknesses and we have emphasized the strengths of the modern forms of budgeting but in education it is often not possible to rationalize operations through concrete terms and on its basis concretize outcomes. For instance, it is well established that integration of technology leads to better learning. But how will you quantify better learning as an output after the budget period? There are also apprehensions that conflicts may lead to negation of the justification for a programme resulting in non allocation of funds. Calculating cost effectiveness may also be difficult as the output in education unlike in industries may not be tangible and assessable, as for instance, learning. However enrolment, retention and percentage of those successfully clearing the programme may be considered as some of the indicators of effectiveness.

At this point we would like you to ponder over certain issues. Enrolment in a programme is definitely an indication of cost effectiveness of a programme. But can enrolment be always equated to a quality programme? For example, there may be Government policy pre-requisiting a particular kind of education/ training for a profession, like B.Ed. for teaching. This can lead to a craze for B.Ed. programmes with mushrooming of institutions offering it. Does this mean that we altogether do away with disciplines that fail to attract sizeable enrolment in favour of such programmes? Also, when budgeting is done annually, the output may not be predictable. At times many years are needed to gauge the success of a programme. Hence ZBB may be used judiciously for plans to be implemented over many years.

Rolling Budget

It is a budget continuously created by adding a further period, which could be a month or a quarter and deducing the earliest period. It involves preparation of targets and plans which are more realistic and certain, especially in regard to price levels, by shortening the period between preparing the budgets. Instead of annual, there would be budgets every month, quarter, or every six months. A rolling budget may be prepared every three months. Four rolling budgets would be prepared in a year in this case. The first three months of the year would be planned in greater details with planning and determining the requirements of working capital and short term resources than the remaining nine months of the year because of the uncertainties in the long term future (Jhamb, 2008). Having to repeat the budget making procedure many times in a year may get tedious but budget for smaller periods may provide more realistic projections.

4.5.1 *Shifting to new budgeting techniques*

Shifting to new methods of budgeting like ZBB may require change in attitude in those engaged in activities and programmes and also in those engaged in preparing the budget. The former group may require persuasion to give up the activities they had been pursuing. Managers may need to perform a tight rope walk while putting across to people and departments that the activity they had been engaged in is no longer required. They will have to be prepared for viewing activities and programmes objectively. They also need to understand that discontinuation of wasteful expenses would help the organization and its employees in the long run. Hence techniques of change management may need to be employed. Those involved in preparing the budget may also have to be persuaded to shift to new techniques. They may also require training, at least an orientation to the new method and for this the management has to invite experts who can provide hands on training.

In many educational institutions control over the budgeting process is often limited as budget preparation is done by the bodies running the institution. There are also other constraints in budgeting. The main issues and problems identified in budgeting in institutions of higher education are: focus on inputs with an overwhelming concern to control spending, rather than to monitor efficiency of responsibility centres as would happen under a performance budget whereby allocations are linked to performance of a unit or to monitor effectiveness of programmes as would happen under a programme budget. The inadequate use of responsibility accounting concepts and lack of proper variance analysis are also matters of concerns. The limitations of cash based budgeting and the need to provide information on costs of operations is essential and prerequisites for budgeting. Often there is a short time perspective for budgets. This is yet another problem. Moreover, the fragmented or non-comprehensive nature of the budgetary process is also a problem. There is a need for a comprehensive and well coordinated approach to budget preparation instead of different departments preparing their own budget (Shand, 1982).

Budget preparation is often a ritual and routine activity in educational institutions but change is apparent as in the budgeting carried out as for instance, in the university libraries in Nigeria, where there has been shift from the incremental budgeting towards Activity Based Budgeting (ABB). This new approach entails building up annual budgets estimates based on programme using the Activity Based Budgeting (ABB) method. This is done to ensure that figures are built up from properly costed activities (Edegbo, 2010).

4.6 Process of Budgeting

Now that you know about the approaches to budgeting, some basic steps to be followed in preparing a budget are discussed below.

Identification of financial resources: Apart from the funds available on a regular basis to the educational institutions, those that can be mobilized also need to be identified. The financial resources available during the budget period have first to be identified and projected. You also need to reflect upon the current financial position of the organization.

Prioritization of needs: Programmes, projects, activities that are to be taken up during the budget period on priority basis have to be identified. However, there is a need to have objectivity while prioritizing the needs.

Evaluating activities: Activities may be evaluated to select those that can fulfill the goals of the organization. Educational activities or programmes may be evaluated on the basis of data collected through the established methods of data collection. Data pertaining to variables such as student enrolment, operational costs like those involved in providing student support services, infrastructural and faculty requirements, transportation costs, etc. need to be collected. Cost benefit analysis for various activities or programmes is thus necessary. With estimation of costs, it has to be decided whether an activity to be continued/undertaken would be cost effective. Previous enrolment figures in an educational programme, socio-economic demand for a programme and other factors can project the future enrolment and hence the cost effectiveness of a programme. Universities have been urged to be financially self sufficient and funds are often not sufficient (see Chapter 1). Therefore, cost effective activities and programmes will have to be prioritized. Activities that have been carried out in the past but have ceased to be economically viable need to be phased out or modified. For instance, a programme with very low enrolment may be taken off or modified in a way that enhances enrolment.

Some educational programmes that may not have high enrolment but have their social and educational values may not be abandoned altogether. Otherwise educational programmes on classical and even regional languages and certain disciplines with high academic but low market value may not be sustained.

Realistic and reasonable: Budget estimates should be realistic and reasonable. It is to be seen that the plans made can be implemented.

Adoption of the Budget: The budget prepared has to be presented for approval to the appropriate body. The budget once approved becomes binding. This process is to be completed before the beginning of the budget period for which the budget has been made.

4.7 Budgetary Control

A budget once prepared has to be implemented monitored and controlled. All these activities together constitute the administration of the budget. It is as important as budget preparation. Monitoring the budget should not be a periodic affair but should be carried out regularly through out the budget period. The Commonwealth Secretariat, (1993) has mentioned certain steps for monitoring budgets in schools and they are also relevant in institutions imparting higher education.

- Check that income and expenditures are in compliance with the budget.
- Check if the budget is balanced in true sense and see whether there is a surplus or deficit fund at the end of the budget period and if there is a possibility of building reserves.
- Assess the budget and its implementation in order to prepare subsequent budgets efficiently.
- Provide continuity in the accounting system as financial accounts are established on the basis of the balance sheet of the previous year and continue as that for the ensuing year.

Budgetary control is a technique that compares the actualities with the budgetary provisions. The differences i.e. the variances are detected (if any) and they are investigated and revision of budget is then carried out. It involves the following steps:

- Actual performance is compared with the budgetary provisions;
- Significant deviations if any are detected and investigated;
- Deviations from the budget (plans) are duly reported;
- Corrective actions such as complying adherence to policies, changing policies and plans, etc, are taken.
- The budget (plan) is revised if variance is due to projections located in the budget.

Why need budgetary control?

Budgetary control is not a fault finding device but it helps in overall monitoring and fulfilment of the goals of the organisation. It has several advantages such as:

- It measures actual performances and detects variances and identifies factors leading to variances.
- It compels management to develop a vision for the organization and make purposes and directions concrete.
- It builds accountability and makes responsibility centers aware of their budgetary responsibilities like targets, means and deadlines.

- It is a means of performance appraisal of units and individuals responsible for carrying out programmes and activities.
- Enables corrective actions to be taken as variances are detected and lead to new plans, objectives and policies.

As long as the actual performance approximately conforms to the budget, no intervention is needed. But it is certainly needed when there are significant deviations.

Budgetary control is the science of planning the budget itself and its utilisation to effect an overall management for business planning and control. Installation of budgetary control system may be done through the following steps (Jhamb, 2008):

- Any system of budgetary control requires a clear perspective of the objectives which may be relating to present products and lines of activity and for the proposed new products and activities.
- **Coordinating the estimates:** Department heads are required to provide estimates of future conditions and activities that will impact the performance of the organisation. At this stage estimates of costs, revenue, resources available are sought from the units of the organisation and then coordinated into an integrated whole.
- **Authority-responsibility relationship:** Responsibilities and functional relationships should be defined through an organisational chart to define the lines of authority and responsibilities of those involved in attaining the objectives of the organisation.
- **Preparation of budget manual:** A document needs to be prepared that specifies the objectives of thc organisation and with the essential information needed for construction, administration and execution of budget. It may also provide for periodical review and the forms and procedures for such reviews for exercising budgetary control.
- **Budgeting administration:** For the overall monitoring of the budgetary process two functionaries are created. They are: budget committee and budget controller.

- ☐ **Budget committee:** It is an advisory committee and looks after the policy matters related to budgeting. It ensures that the budgets are realistic and are coordinated well. It collects, scrutinises and reviews the functional budget estimates; recommends and/ approves suggestions in functional budgets, reviews and adopts the final budget, collects and reviews periodic performance report from various units, identifies deviations and takes corrective measures if deviations are detected.
- ☐ Budget controller directs the budget programme.

- **Budget period:** It is the time for which a budget is prepared and implemented. It is usually the accounting year subdivided into four quarters or twelve months. A continuous or rolling budget is a twelve month budget prepared twice or thrice a year. Frequent budget preparation may give more accurate budget but are prone to ministerial errors. Another method is to prepare basic budget and current budget. The former is for a long period of time. A current budget is used over a short period of time and is related to current conditions.
- **Budget procedure:** It involves the determination of key factors also called critical factor, whose influence must be evaluated properly as they influence the functional budget. Key factors in an educational organisation may be enrolment, cost of developing programmes, etc. Information on expected increase or decrease in enrolment, raise in fee and the like are therefore needed. The policies of the organisation need to be communicated for budgeting.

4.7.1 *Variance Analysis*

As you have read earlier, variances may be detected in the planned and actual levels and an analysis of variance may then be done. As underlined by Chandra (2004) variances may be of the types:

- Variances due to differences in planned and actual levels of sales called marketing variances or volume variances. For instance if an educational programme is launched and the sale of prospectus was planned as 300 but in actuality is 150. This will lead to lesser sales revenue.

- Variance caused by unit prices (unit costs) is called price variance and this type of variances caused by efficient or inefficient utilization of inputs are called efficiency variances.

4.8 Flexible Budgeting

As mentioned earlier, a budget is a tool for planning as well as for financial management. The original budget prepared before the budget period starts may project for instance, enrolment in under graduate course in History as 500 and accordingly depicts the volume of production of educational resources, costs involved and the income from the fees, sale of prospectus and educational materials, etc. Suppose a policy suddenly comes into effect that teacher education in particular states at the secondary level shall be stopped for some years, the enrolment in teacher education programmes would then suddenly dip. Similarly enrolment may suddenly rise in some programmes. Or the institution may find unexpected expenses/income. A static budget will not permit the necessary changes. But a flexible budget tries to adjust the static budget to the actual output say for instance, higher or lower enrolment and accordingly changes the related considerations. Therefore, a flexible budget is used to accommodate the uncertainties and variances in the planned level and the actual level of activities carried out. A difficulty often encountered is that money has to be spent in a particular financial year within specific parameters like standard funds. If it can be carried forth to the next financial year or if viring it to other budgetary heads (switching over expenditure with funds meant for one head being spent on another) is permitted has to be seen (Donnelly, 2003). This would help in reducing the rigidity associated with the strict monitoring of the budget.

A flexible budget takes into account the variable costs that are proportionate to the level of the activity and the total fixed costs that are independent of the level of the activity. It can thus accommodate varying levels of income and expenses and provides a meaningful basis of comparison. However it is not advisable that changes in the budget are made every now and then.

4.9 Budgeting with Sensitivity

In an educational institution, budgeting requires making hard choices as prioritizing activities, suspending non profitable activities, preferring activities that bring in funds and the like. This could lead to conflicts and debates. Interdepartmental conflicts and unhealthy competition could also arise. For instance, doing away with courses and programme that do not have much market value could be a hard and controversial decision. Besides, budget serves as a tool for planning and also for performance evaluation. Unutilized and underutilized funds, wastage of resources, failure to meet the dead lines, etc. become transparent and may lead to a blame game. Hence, budgeting has to be done but with a great deal of prudence.

4.10 Summary

A budget is a tool for exercising control over financial transactions of the organization and reflects the aspirations of the organization and the means available to realize them. It includes mainly the organization's expected incomes and proposed expenditures over a certain period of time. It is thus a comprehensive and coordinated documented plan of the accepted expenditures and revenue of an organization expressed in financial terms. It is prepared for a definite period of time called budget period, which is usually for one year but it may be broken down into smaller periods. It is a basis for the expenditures to be incurred and enlists the resources (revenue) and the expenses to be undertaken during the budget period. The budget is not merely a statement of income and expenses but if made and implemented well it can serve as a tool for management by objectives.

The essential considerations while budgeting are the goals, objectives and the policies of the institution. Unambiguous projections that can be translated into fiscal terms are also needed. Estimates should also be realistic and objective and data used should be based on the accounting system of the institution. Decentralized budgeting with wider participation in budget preparation leads to its better implementation.

A Budget is basically of two types—Operating budget and Finance budget. Operating budgets pertain to the impact of operating decisions mainly like production, sales and purchases. It includes different types of budgets like the sales budget, production budget, purchase budget, etc. The financial budget depicts the financial implications of the operating budget, i.e. the expected inflow and outflow of cash. It includes the capital expenditure budget, the cash budget and the budgeted balance sheet.

A budget can be prepared in different ways. Traditionally prepared budget is easier to prepare. But it is prepared on the basis of the budget of the previous year with some increment in the expenses planned. However, it emphasizes only the past activities and has little scope for changes. It allocates expenses into categories of inputs and summarizes expenses in gross terms. It is thus input oriented. Program budget is a fiscal plan related to the programs or the activities such as student support, evaluation, etc., undertaken by an organization. It establishes the programmes, their objectives, costs, i.e. resources and the expected results. Performance budgeting is similar to program budgeting but it emphasizes costing i.e. cost of a programme. Statements of missions, goals and objectives included in this approach justify the investments. ZBB starts with zero as the base line. Each programme or activity has to be justified and each year a budget from a zero base has to be constructed by providing new objectives, evaluation criteria and justifications.

Irrespective of the approach to budgeting, the process of budgeting involves steps like identification of financial resources, prioritization of needs, and estimation of costs, preparation and finally presentation of the budget for approval by the appropriate body. This process is to be completed before the beginning of the budget period for which the budget has been made. As important as preparing a budget is the budgetary control. It is a technique that compares the actual results with the budgetary provisions. The differences i.e. the variances are detected (if any) and they are investigated and there is revision of budget. Ideally variance should be less but still a budget needs to be flexible. A flexible budget is used to accommodate the uncertainties and variances in the planned level and the actual level of activities carried out. Budget preparation undoubtedly requires cost analyses for continuing/starting institutional initiatives, prioritizing needs and phasing out unprofitable activities. Nevertheless consideration for programmes with disciplinary value, even if they have low enrolment is required. Sensitivity is also needed to avoid conflicts while prioritizing programmes for budgetary allocation.

4.11 Self Assessment

4.11.1 *Questions*

Answer the following questions:

(i) What is a budget?

(ii) Prepare a sales budget for an educational institution.

(iii) Prepare a cash budget for an educational institution.

(iv) Why should budget preparation involve teachers?

(v) What are the weaknesses of traditional budgeting?

(vi) How does a ZBB overcome the weaknesses of traditional budgeting?

(vii) Explain the importance of budgetary control.

4.11.2 *Clues*

(i) A budget is a fiscal expression, rather a comprehensive and coordinated plan, expressed in financial terms for the operations to be undertaken and resources available in an enterprise for a specific period in the future (See Section 4.3).

(ii) & (iii) refer to the examples given in the text (See Section 4.4).

(iv) Budget preparation is an act of planning and a mechanism of fulfilling the strategies formed for attaining the objectives and goals of the institution. A team with teachers would be able to take into account the ground realities and the budget prepared will also have wider acceptability.

(v) It may suffer from a number of limitations such as:

- The previous financial year's budget is considered to be ideal and a model basing on which the next budget is to be built.
- It may encourage units to demand for increased budget every year.

- It will not encourage units to economise as next year's budget would definitely bring more money.
- It cannot accommodate new activities like new courses or new level of an existing activity as for example sudden increase in enrolment due to relaxation in eligibility conditions for a particular programme. Therefore new initiatives may be discouraged.
- High or low funding for a particular activity will continue in the next year without any scope for rectifying it to the right amount.

(vi) Prioritization of activities is done in terms of their ability to fulfill the goals of the organization and cost involved and then only funds are allocated. Thus there is objectivity in budgeting. Unlike incremental budgeting, future rather than past is important and it can accommodate changes. Moreover, only the economically viable projects are prioritized (See Section 4.5).

(vii) It is a technique that compares the actual results with the budgetary provisions. The differences i.e. the variances are detected (if any) and they are investigated and the concerned people then carry out revision of budget (See Section 4.7).

4.12 Activities

You may carry out these activities for gaining a better understanding of this chapter.

1. "A budget helps in identifying needs, control expenditure and ensure accountability. It also provides opportunity to staff members to articulate the financial requirements" (Enaohwo, 1990). Critically examine the budget of an educational institution in the light of this statement.
2. From an educational institution find out the extent of participation of teachers in the budget preparation and whether they have received any training in budget preparation.
3. Study the budget prepared by any educational institution. Examine the approach to budgeting.
4. Find out from any two institutions of higher education about their approach to budget preparation and the reasons thereof.

5. Organize a debate on the following topic:

   "Programmes that do not earn revenue for the educational institution should be weeded out through result oriented budgeting in favour of only those that bring in revenue for the institution."

6. Discuss with your colleagues/peers about the role that student representatives could play in budget preparation of a college/university and its advantages and disadvantages.

References

Bhatnagar, R.P. and Agrawal, V. (1997). *Education Administration, Supervision, Planning and Financing*. Meerut: Surya Publications.

Chandra, P. (2003). *Finance Sense – Finance for Non-finance Executives*. New Delhi: Tata Mc Graw Hill Publishing Company.

Commonwealth Secretariat (1993). *Better Schools, Resource Materials for School Heads in Africa*. Module 5—Financial Management. Commonwealth Secretariat, UNESCO: London.

Donnelly, J. (2003). *Managing Urban Schools–Leading from the Front*. London : Kogan Page.

Edegbo, W.O. (2010). Budget preparation, approval, and implementation in university libraries in Nigeria. *Library Philosophy and Practice, BNET* Retrieved on 20/9/10 from http://findarticles.com/p/articles/mi_7005/is_2010_June/ai_n54641911/pg_5/?tag=content;col1

Enaohwo, J.O. (1990). *Economics of Education and the Planning Challenge*. New Delhi: Anmol Publications.

Jhamb, H.V. (2008). *Fundamentals of Management Accounting*. India: Anne Books India.

Orlosky, D.E. McCleary, L.E., Webb, L.D. (1984). *Educational Administration Today*. New York : MacMillan Publishing Company.

Pandey, I.M. (1983). *Financial Management*. Delhi : Vikas Publishing House Pvt. Ltd..

Shand, D.A. (1982). Budgeting in Tertiary Educational Institutions: an Analysis. *Journal of Higher Education Policy and Management*, 4 (2) 185-194.

Young, R.D. (2003). Performance-Based Budget Systems. Public Policy & Practice. Retrieved on 12.10.11 from www.iopa.sc.edu/ejournal/assets/performance%20based%20budgets.pdf

Websites (Websites my not be permanent)

http://www.economywatch.com/budget/types/zero-based.html Retrieved on 24/12/08

<http://www.duncanwil.co.uk/budg.html Retrieved on 24/12/08>

http://www.ncvo-vol.org.uk/sfp/finance/index.asp?id=481 Retrieved on 24/12/08

http://www.ci.concord.ca.us/CITYGOV/finance/pbb.htm Retrieved on 24/12/08

http://www.informaworld.com/smpp/content~db=all~content=a746539042 Retrieved on 22/9.10

5

Utilization of Resources and Monitoring Financial Transactions

5.1 Introduction

It is important for administrators of educational institutions to be adept in managing financial resources of their institutions but this requires specialized knowledge and skills. In India expenditure on the education sector is lower than that required in the majority of the states. But that is only part of the problem. It is not only the total allocation but its utilization and management which determine the outcome (De & Endow, 2008). Hence, there is the need for awareness of certain general principles as well as of certain precautionary measures that are to be adopted so as to ensure that the funds collected from the various sources can be safeguarded and expended in a judicious manner. There is also the need to make financial plans, prioritize needs and perform cost benefit analysis prior to incurring expenditure. The general principles of financial management in an educational institution have therefore been discussed in this chapter. Two important aspects of financial management—utilization of resources and monitoring assets have also been discussed in this chapter. Thus the chapter is about the basic framework of financial management.

5.2 Objectives

This chapter aims to enable you to:

- Explain the mechanisms of efficient utilization of financial resources;
- Discuss the principles of financial management; and
- Explain how financial transactions and assets of the institution can be monitored.

5.3 Utilization of Financial Resources

It is true that financial management being a complex area it should be left to the specialists in this field. But successful management of an educational institution requires the knowhow of the basics of financial management. Why is it so? This is because the leaders of an educational institution are accountable for the utilization of funds and their safe custody. Even minor slip-ups and oversights may have serious repercussions. Moreover, educational institutions of our country often face acute shortage of financial resources. Educational managers are therefore urged to be entrepreneurs and mobilize resources for the institution. Earlier making a profit by any educational institution was unacceptable but now the outlook is changing. Although profiteering should never be the motive of an educational organization but generating funds for its growth and development is being encouraged. Educational institutions, especially those imparting higher education need to be self reliant. Generating surplus funds, diverting it for the growth of the institution and saving the rest by educational institutions are no longer considered to be sacrilegious. We have discussed this in the first chapter.

With growing private participation and globalization and reducing government support, educational organizations will need sound financial management to survive. Therefore, proper planning, decision making and controlling the financial assets would be needed. Hence the funds available have to be safeguarded from all sorts of misuse as well as wastage and non utilization. Therefore, plans and programmes need to be developed and implemented with full care. On one hand it has to be ensured that funds are not misused and on the other hand it is equally important to ensure that the funds available do not lie unused. Educational managers may have to oversee the processes of budgeting, accounting, preparation of financial reports, internal auditing and other such activities. They are also responsible for investment of funds, managing associated risks, mobilizing resources, working out financial details in case of partnerships and the like. Therefore, educational managers have to equip themselves with the basics of financial management.

This is all the more relevant for academics from disciplines other than finance related ones.

Prudent management of financial resources is essential. What sort of prudence is expected of a manager of an educational institution? Financial management implies administration and the maintenance of the financial assets of the institution and thereby planning and controlling the financial assets. Decisions are to be made and one has to remember that even small differences may snowball into uncontrollable situations. Prudence in financial management may be exercised by posing three basic questions: '*why*', '*when*', and '*how*' for any activity having financial implications. The first question—'why' would lead to justifications for an activity to be undertaken. This would be done through an objective analysis of the needs and developing a sound rationale for the activity. The next question—'when', would lead to prioritization of needs and activities and suggest when it is to be carried out. Thereby the urgency of the activity can be determined. The third question, 'how' would lead to an exploration of resources available and also of the means of carrying out the activity and selecting the economically viable means and determining the time frame within which it would have to be accomplished. This will ensure that the funds available are prudently spent and also saved. Answering these questions would require the manager to closely monitor the fund inflow as well as outflow (Bose, 2007). S/he would be concerned with how to minimize costs without compromising on quality. It would also be necessary to pay due importance to the accounts (assets, liabilities and net worth) in determining the financial position of the institution. Besides the manager is ultimately responsible for the various economic assets—fixed (property, plant and equipment) and liquid assets (cash and deposits) of the institution. Thus adopting certain measures would ensure prudence in financial management. These measures have been discussed in the following sections:

5.3.1 *Functioning within the framework of financial policies and rules*

An important precondition for prudent utilization of funds is that educational managers function within the established framework of financial policies and rules. This can safeguard to a great extent against financial irregularities and mismanagement. Financial rules govern several aspects including maintenance of financial records, inflow and outflow of funds. Awareness of policies and rules pertaining to inflow of funds such as fee, fines, grants, etc. and outflow like salary, student support services, purchases, investments, etc. is needed for financial management. As an educational manager, one has to know about the entitlements of the institution regarding public funds. Information related to the type of grants for which the institution is eligible and the other sources of funds. When to apply for grants, the amount due, the income that can be generated from fee, maintaining proper account of the money collected and spent, custody of funds, investments, etc. should be governed by the established policies and rules. Rules pertaining to House Rent Allowance, conveyance, medical reimbursements, various allowances enjoyed, travel grants, etc. should be considered to be inviolable for managing the transactions within the organization. It is also important that the funds and grants collected for a prescribed purpose are utilized for the same purpose and accounted for accordingly by the institution. Special permission may be required for diverting funds to heads other than those for which they were actually intended. Expenditures undertaken and investment of profits by educational institutions may also be governed by established policies and rules. It has to be ensured that in an academic institution, expenses on non academic activities and lavishness have to be contained.

5.3.2 *Maintaining accounts*

It is necessary to maintain accounts as per standard practices of accounting. There should be clear and to the point reporting that includes the details of day to day financial transactions. For activities such as budgeting, approval, funding, review, validation, auditing, etc., maintaining accounts is important. Thus accounting is the backbone of financial management. We shall not go into the details of maintaining accounts as a separate chapter has been devoted to it.

5.3.3 *Prioritization*

We have already mentioned that educational institutions generally face shortage of financial resources. The grants received from the government and the fee collected may be barely enough to meet the expenses of an institution desiring to provide quality education. Hence, there is a need to prioritize activities to be undertaken. Fiscal plans are at times prepared on the basis of what has been already continuing in the organization. Consequently a status quo is maintained as far as the nature of activities is considered. However there is a need to analyze the activities in terms of the results i.e. the economic gains that would be reaped from them. Of course, there could be other factors that need to be taken into consideration, for instance, academic value of a discipline like a classical language, pressing socio-economic needs for a programme to which an institution of higher education, as an integral part of the community has to respond, etc. For instance, an awareness programme on AIDS or disaster management may be accorded priority even if financial returns are not very high. Student support services may have to be prioritised so as to enhance retention. Investment in technologies that would have long term benefits may also be considered to be important. Prioritisation and decision-making are crucial to financial management and it has been rightly pointed out by Law & Glover (2000) that these processes are often indicative of an organization's prevailing management culture and the constraints it faces, especially in a resource-starved climate. Thus the long term gains that would accrue from an activity have to be considered.

5.3.4 *Analyzing benefits and assessing risks*

As suggested in the chapter on budgeting, it would be prudent to weigh the costs and the benefits of introducing a new course of action. The new course of action could be starting something new, altering an ongoing activity or suspending an ongoing activity. An analytical approach needs to be adopted and it is also important to assess the financial risks involved. This helps us to determine the value for money. The concept of 'value for money' implies that money is to be spent in a way that ensures substantial returns from it. In other words, the benefits from the investment should be optimum. An efficient school is one, which provides excellent 'value for money' because it makes good use of all its available resources to achieve the best possible educational outcomes for all its pupils. This requires cost benefit analysis that offers ways of assessing the outcome of expenditure on the basis of estimates made by including the costs of all the elements of a proposed investment. For this 'Direct' as well as 'Indirect' expenses are to be taken into account (Law & Glover, 2000). The same assumption would hold good for planning and prioritizing in institutions of higher education.

The managers have to consider the 'Value for money' before a project is undertaken. A cost benefit analysis if carried out before undertaking the project will tell us about the value for money, i.e. whether the project undertaken will generate profit for the organization. However, profit in an educational institution may not just be monetary but also in terms of social responsibility carried out and reputation earned.

You may study the following examples:

1. For investment in imparting training to the employees of an educational institution for developing computer literacy, an important consideration may be that such investment could do away with the need to outsource to external agencies work to be carried out with the help of computer or hire help for it. The added benefit would be that the teachers could impart computer-assisted instruction to the students.
2. An educational institution intends to offer a new course of study, say a programme—diploma in peace education. Although peace education is needed in the modern conflict ridden world, nevertheless, an analysis has to be carried out in terms of the factors like the following:
    - Cost involved in developing the programme, through activities like planning and developing the curriculum, developing academic resources;

- Cost involved in implementing the programme (through estimation of costs that would be involved in engaging academic and supporting staff to deliver the programme through various media, in conducting evaluation, etc.);
- The nature of the target group and expected number that would enroll in the programme;
- Whether the fee collected from the students would be sufficient to meet the expenses involved in developing and implementing the programme;
- The sources of funds apart from fees for the programme, exploring for instance possibilities of getting sponsors for the programme.

Analyzing along such lines would give an idea about the costs, expected returns and the risks involved.

3. An institution finds that lessening the weight of practical component from 50% to 30% for a particular academic programme could cut down the costs of offering the programme. Before taking a decision pertinent questions need to be asked like—whether lessening the practical component would compromise skill development of learners; whether the decision would affect employability of those passing out; whether this would affect the credibility of the programme and the reputation of the institution; and the like.
4. For designing and developing courseware some institutions may outsource some of the work instead of getting it done internally. In this case factors like resources available in-house and the deadlines for completing the work are important. If outsourcing leads to expenses but quality, and is economic in the long run in comparison to recruiting more faculties, the decision may be in favour of outsourcing.

Hence, value for money of a project is an important consideration for efficient and economic utilization of the funds available. Otherwise the manager would be taking a risk while making investment. However, as you find in some of the example, for determining value for money, monetary gains should not be the sole consideration.

Law & Glover (2000) outlined a three stage rational planning approach focused on meeting organizational aims in cost effective ways. The stages are:

- Agree on and articulate aims and priorities focused on organizational goals;
- Collect and analyze data for choices which are based on prior experiences.
- Select the best set of actions to achieve specified aims and objectives.

At times certain investments are made but soon it is found that the expenditure has been wasteful. For instance, investing in training the faculty to use computers for teaching but not ensuring adequate access to computers in the institution would make the expenditure wasteful. Unutilized or underutilized equipments of Information and Communication Technology (ICT) in some educational institutions make the investment wasteful. For instance, there is a recurrent pattern in investment in ICT based initiatives in institutions imparting distant education. Huge amounts are spent on infrastructure for ICT, which eventually remain underutilized (Suri, 2008).

5.3.5 *Linking strategic planning with financial planning*

Strategic planning is as important in educational institutions as in the corporate sector for achieving the goals. The strategic plan spells out the mission that in turn elaborates the scope, objectives and strategies to attain the objectives. Financial management is an essential means for attaining the goals of the institution. The goal of the institution may be to provide quality education at affordable prices, which may also be the raison d'etre of the institution. The objectives, which are the goals specified, may be for instance be to attain a growth of 15% in enrolment, to integrate ICT in teaching and learning, to provide student support services, ensure timely declaration of results, etc. Means of assessment of the progress made towards the attainment of the goals may also be included. Financial planning could involve appraisal of the current financial position, make financial projections and outline financial requirements and plan the extent and timing of expenses during a period. All these activities maybe an integral part of the strategic planning, i.e. linked to the objectives, the priorities and the resources of the organisation.

5.3.6 *Decision making*

- We have already mentioned that financial decisions have to be taken as per the established policies and rules (see 5.3.1), the need to have accounts as the backbone of financial management (see 5.3.2), the need for prioritising while expending (see 5.3.3), to carry out cost benefit analysis for decision-making (see 5.3.4) and to ensure that decisions regarding investments and expenditures help in achieving the organisation's strategic plans and objectives (see 5.3.5). Thus the measures outlined so far for prudence in financial management are important for financial decisions.

Law & Glover (2000) have mentioned 4 Es as bases for financial planning. They are:

- **Economy:** Obtaining quality products/services at minimum cost.
- **Effectiveness:** Matching outcomes/results of the activity against the objectives/resources invested.
- **Efficiency:** Securing outcomes at minimum cost.
- **Equity:** Ensuring a fair distribution of resources to support the learning activities.

A manager of an educational institution may be responsible for acquisition and allocation of funds and utilization of funds. Even huge amounts of funds may not fulfill the desired goals if poorly managed. Techniques like comparative financial statement, budgets, ratio analysis, variance analysis, cost- volume, profit analysis, etc. help in the decision making process. These tools help in evaluating the profitability of the project. The manager also has to forecast the funds required and estimate the sources from which they would be available. S/he also has to be concerned with planning and forecasting of production, sales and level of inventory. For this the knowledge of how much funds would be coming from which sources at what time is required.

Decisions relating to finance in industries and business houses differ from that of an educational institution. Educational institutions may have to take decisions such as:

Financing Decision: It is important to decide when, where from and how to acquire funds to meet the institution's investment needs. The sources from which funds may be mobilized have to be explored. We have discussed this in details in the first chapter. Although it is stressed that planning and decision making should be based on cost effectiveness of projects and activities but in the field of education results are often intangible and available following a long wait. However enrolment, retention and success rate in a programme are important factors. Higher enrolments plough back the investment made in developing and delivering the programme. Rate of retention and success rate i.e. percentage of pass outs and their employability determine the effectiveness of the project.

Investment Decision: The institution may have scarce resources that must be allocated among competing uses. On one hand the funds may be used to create additional capacity which in turn generates additional revenue and profits. For instance, starting new departments and programmes are some such measure. On the other hand, some investments may not yield immediate gains but after a period of time the benefits are apparent. For instance, investment in providing student support services like tutoring, counselling, etc. may facilitate retention and better achievement, visible over the years. Decisions have to be taken after weighing the pros and cons. Projects that are initiated but get aborted after initial investments, equipments purchased but not utilised to their full potential lead to drainage of resources.

5.3.7 *Budgeting*

Preparing a budget is an important activity for financial management. A budget should be prepared realistically keeping in view the sources of funds and expenses to be incurred during a financial year. The budget prepared should serve as a tool that assesses the financial performances and helps in monitoring the financial resources of the institution. Funds are provided to universities on the basis of the budget prepared. We have discussed budgeting as a strategy for financial management in the chapter devoted exclusively to budgeting.

5.3.8 *Utilizing physical resources with prudence*

Apart from the financial resources, physical resources of the organisation also have to be utilized with prudence. Unutilized assets like land, building, equipments indicate poor management of resources. We have discussed the need for utilization of such resources in the first chapter.

5.4 Monitoring Financial Transactions and Safeguarding Resources

Financial resources in educational institutions are often scarce and are often susceptible to misuse. Hence there is a need to monitor all financial transactions throughout the financial year. The major transactions include inflow of financial resources from the various sources and also the outflow of funds as expenditures. There is need to monitor the inflow so that the right amount reaches the right place at the right time. The outflow should also be based on sound decisions. It is to be ensured that for the money paid, services/goods are received on time. Monitoring is also needed to ensure that financial transactions are within the framework of financial policies, rules and regulations and also in keeping with the budgetary provisions. Monitoring of resources in the perspective of the budget prepared is needed on a regular basis to minimize variations. Continuous monitoring and appropriate forecasting of output during the specified period are essential to identify significant deviations from plans and take necessary and immediate corrective actions like reducing or postponing expenditure, carrying out virement (transfer of funds for one account to another with the due approval of authorities during a budget period), and the like. It is particularly important to have an accurate picture of expenditure and receipts towards the end of the financial year. There may also be the need for preparing and submitting Financial Report as an integral part of monitoring resources and overall financial management. These reports draw on information regarding forecasts of outturn (output during a budget period) and explicit reasons of variances.

5.4.1 *Safeguarding resources*

Even minor errors in financial transactions can lead to huge loss of funds and invite penalties. Therefore, the manager has to take certain precautions while undertaking financial transactions. The list of the financial activities, procedures, etc., is too long and hence precautions too many. Some of the precautions are the following:

Maintaining records accurately

Financial information has to be recorded regularly, completely and accurately. The financial information may comprise the following:

- **Information pertaining to revenue:** The various sources of income, be it public or private, and the amount of money received there from, is to be recorded along with the date in the accounting system.
- **Information pertaining to expenditure:** The exact amount of funds paid or promised to be paid, the purpose, date and other details have to be recorded regularly. It is desirable that expense on a broad head are analysed and that on individual items are recorded. For instance, for expenses on computers, those on computers, back up facilities, furniture for these, etc. are mentioned separately.

Safe custody of funds

Ensuring security of funds is the prime responsibility of the managers. Only those authorized should have an access to the funds (Commonwealth Secretariat, 1993). Cash, cheque books and other financial documents should be guarded against theft, forgery, pests, burglary, etc. A physical inventory of all items that can be inventoried must be carried out regularly and any discrepancies must be promptly reported and investigated.

Access to any forms or on-line systems that can be used to alter financial records of the institution must be safeguarded from tampering.

While receiving funds, the amount received in cash or check/ demand draft should be verified. The cheque/draft should be checked for the following:

- The date on the cheque should be checked.
- The amount mentioned in words and figure should match.
- The cheque should preferably be an account payee one.
- The cheque/draft should have been signed properly by the payer.
- In case of any overwriting on the cheque there should be initials of the payer.
- The name of payee (receiving person/institution) should have been written properly.
- Validity of the cheque should not have been over.

Precautions related to withdrawal of funds

There are also certain precautions regarding withdrawal of money as for instance,

- No space should be left blank while writing the amount in figures/words, which should be written clearly.
- Overwriting should be minimal and accompanied by initials of the signatories.
- Counterfoil should be maintained and the reason for withdrawal of funds should be mentioned on it.
- It should be ensured that the requisite funds are there in the account since bouncing of cheques may lead to penalty for the signatories.
- Proper count of the leaves of the cheque book should be kept and they should be used serially.

- For lost cheque/cheque books, the bank should be instructed to stop payment to prevent wrong payment.

The banking forms should be filled carefully and copies of deposit forms (pay-in-slips) should be retained (Commonwealth Secretariat, 1993). While depositing money in the bank account it may be ensured that the bank employee signs the counterfoil of the deposit slip. The document with details of transactions needs to be updated regularly. Bank statements must be received on a regular basis and reconciled with the amount mentioned in the ledger and the counterfoils. Any discrepancy should be brought to the notice of the bank manager.

5.4.2 *Internal controls*

Managers of educational institutions need to be careful to prevent frauds and see that errors are minimum. Frauds could be due to falsifying or altering the record of financial transactions, omissions in recording transactions, embezzlement of funds, etc. At times unintentional errors may also lead to incorrect financial statements. Internal controls through techniques such as internal check and internal auditing are therefore necessary to monitor and direct the resources for the attainment of the objectives and goals of the institutions. We have discussed this in details in the chapter on auditing.

5.5 Guiding Principles of Financial Management

The discussion carried out in the previous section will be recapitulated and concretized in this section as the principles that guide the major processes related to financial management. The principles are:

- All legitimate sources of funds should be tapped. The right amount should flow in at the right time from the right places.
- Designated purpose of government grants must be met. Using funds provided for one purpose for some other activity is to be avoided unless special permission for the same has been obtained from the competent authorities.
- Assessing cost effectiveness of a project before undertaking it will give the full value for money. This

will reduce depletion of funds in activities that are economically unsound.

- All activities should be within the purview of financial rules, policies and guidelines.
- All the procurements must be conducted on a fair and competitive basis. Comparing the price quotations from different bidders and ensuring that dealings are fair and transparent are needed.
- The lowest offer (price) should be accepted as a general rule except when there are good reasons to the contrary. However, lowest bidding should not be the only consideration. Quality, reputation of the provider, time within which delivery would be made are some of the other considerations. Proper records of quotations, tenders etc. need to be maintained and these must be open for reviews. If the lowest bidding is rejected, the reasons thereof should also be recorded.
- Financial assets should be safeguarded from all sorts of misuse. Framing rules to prevent the unauthorized use of the assets of the institution is necessary.
- Accounts should be maintained as per the generally accepted principles of accounting.
- Auditing and reporting should be done on a regular basis by competent people.
- Budgeting as per modern concepts of budgeting that take into consideration rationale for expenditure.
- An institution should operate within the framework of the budget prepared. Budgetary control is necessary.
- In case of budgetary variances, the same should be examined and corrective measured should be taken.

Using computers

Using computers helps data storage in a safe manner, easy retrieval, processing, and sharing. Softwares such as financial management solutions help in activities related to core financials, payrolls, records management, streamline accounting, managing grants and other incomes, billing systems, preparing budget, analysis of variance between budget estimates and the actual, etc. They may also have an easy-to-navigate interface that can be easily customized as per needs. Complying with financial policies, rules and regulations and reporting requirements, accounting with accuracy, managing payrolls, etc. become simpler with these softwares.

5.6 Summary

Financial resources of an organization need to be managed with prudence. On one hand it has to be ensured that funds are not misused and on the other hand it is equally important to ensure that the funds available do not lie unused. Prudence in financial management may be exercised by posing three basic questions: 'why', 'when', and 'how' for any activity having financial implications. The first question—'why' would lead to justifications for an activity to be undertaken, carried out through an objective analysis of the need for the activity. The question—'when', leads to prioritization of needs. The third question, 'how' leads to an exploration of resources available for carrying out the activity and selecting the economically viable means and determining the time frame within which it would have to be accomplished.

It is necessary for managers to adopt certain measures for managing finance with prudence. These measures include functioning within the framework of established financial policies, rules and regulations; maintaining accounts as per standard practices of accounting; prioritization of needs; carrying out cost benefit analysis to determine the value for money for a particular course of action; linking financial planning and decision making with the organisation's strategic plans and objectives; budgeting realistically keeping in view the sources of funds and expenses to be incurred during a financial year and implementing it properly; utilizing physical assets adequately.

There is a need to monitor all financial transactions throughout the financial year. There is need to monitor the inflow so that the right amount reaches the right place at the right time. The outflow of funds should also be based on sound decisions. The managers also have to take certain precautions while undertaking financial transactions like maintaining accounts properly for information pertaining to revenue and expenses, keeping funds safe by taking adequate precautions while receiving funds and making withdrawals and having proper internal control.

Some of the principles of financial management include tapping all legitimate sources of funds, seeing that designated purpose of government grants are met, assessing cost effectiveness of a project before undertaking it; ensuring that all activities are within the purview of financial rules, policies and guidelines; seeing that all the procurements are conducted on a fair and competitive basis; safeguarding financial assets from misuse; accounting as per generally accepted principles of accounting. Auditing and reporting regularly; having sound system of budgeting and budgetary control; and the like.

5.7 Self Assessment

5.7.1 *Questions*

Answer the following questions:

1. Why do we need prioritization of needs for undertaking expenditures?
2. For decision making in financial matters, state the important considerations.
3. Give an example to explain the concept of 'value for money'.
4. Explain any four precautions necessary for activities related to the receipt of funds.

5.7.2 *Clues*

1. Funds may not be sufficient to meet all the aspirations of the institution, hence prioritization of needs and aspirations becomes necessary and those that have more weight in fulfilling the mission of the institution may be prioritized.
2. Alternatives and options available need to be explored for carrying out an activity and the most economic ones may be selected, of course keeping quality requirements

in view. The process adopted must be efficient to minimize wastages due to duplication, overlapping, etc.

3. Values for money refers to the returns from a project undertaken. If it is more than the investment, then there is value for money. For instance when an investment is made on an auditorium, there may be value for money if it is used regularly and rented when not used by the institution.
4. No space should be left blank while writing the amount in figures/words, which should be written clearly; Overwriting should be avoided and those unavoidable may be accompanied by initials of the signatories; Counterfoil should be maintained and the reason for withdrawal of funds should be mentioned on it. It should be ensured that the requisite funds are there in the account since bouncing of cheques may lead to penalty for the signatories.

5.8 Activities

1. Interview the financial managers of a school and an institution imparting higher education to determine the measures adopted for safeguarding the physical assets of the institution.
2. Find out from a school and an educational institution imparting higher education about the utilization of its physical resources like surplus land, auditorium, etc.
3. Interview the financial managers of a school and an institution imparting higher education to determine the measures adopted for exerting internal control.

References

Bose, S.(2007). Principles & Strategies for financial management. *School governance and financial management*. PG Diploma in School Leadership and Management. New Delhi: IGNOU.

Bhatnagar, R.P. & Agrawal, V. (1997). *Educational Administration, Supervision, Planning and Financing*. Meerut : Surya Publications.

Commonwealth Secretariat (1993). Better Schools, *Resource Materials for School Heads in Africa*. Module 5—Financial Management. Commonwealth Secretariat, UNESCO: London.

De, A. & Endow, T. (2008). Public Expenditure on Education in India: Recent Trends and Outcomes. *Research Consortium on Educational Outcomes and Poverty (RECOUP) Working Paper No.18*. Retrieved on 19.8.11 from http://recoup.educ.cam.ac.uk/publications/WP18-ADfin.pdf

Law, S. & Glover, D. (2000). *Educational Leadership and Learning–Practice, Policy and Research*. Philadelphia: Open University Press.

Suri, S. (2008). Imperatives of the information society: a critical perspective on ICT policy and practice in distance education. Paper presented at the *5th Pan COL*, London July 2008.

